Integral Deep Listening:
Accessing Your Life Compass

I0429740

Joseph Dillard

Integral Deep Listening Press
Berlin, Germany 2014

Also by Joseph Dillard

Dreamworking:
How to Use Your Dreams for Creative Problem Solving
Transformational Dreamwork:
Toward an Integral Approach to Deep Listening
Waking Up: How to Use Integral Deep Listening to Transform Your Life
Seven Octaves of Enlightenment: Integral Deep Listening Pranayama
Integral Deep Listening Interviewing Techniques
Integral Deep Listening Practitioner
Integral Deep Listening and Healing
Integral Deep Listening and Meditation
Dream Sociometry
Understanding the Dream Sociogram
Integral Deep Listening: Awakening Your Life Compass
Transcending Your Monkey Mind:
The Five Trees and Meditation
Ending Nightmares for Good
Integral Deep Listening Case Studies
Light from Heaven: Deep Listening to Near Death Experiences.
Words and Concepts that Are and Are Not Conducive to Enlightenment:
Understanding Principles Fundamental to Integral Deep Listening
Dream Yoga: Der weg der Träume

Table of Contents

Introduction

Would you like to be able to interpret any dream that you have? Would you like to understand not only why you have nightmares but how to make them go away forever? Would you like to understand why your life is sometimes like a bad dream and how to change soap opera and nightmarish life events into a good and fulfilling reality? Would you like to learn how to find and follow your inner, or life compass? Would you like to discover what sickness, adversity, and accidents have to teach you? Would you like to learn a powerful method of prevention to head off physical and emotional stress before they show up as problems in your waking life?

Integral Deep Listening (IDL) is a type of dream yoga, or yoga of wakefulness. It is about learning how to wake up out of delusion and misery in your daily life. Rather than focusing on lucid dreaming, as most dream yogas do, IDL emphasizes lucid *living,* waking up out of your waking delusions. When you do so you bring a broader, more inclusive consciousness to both your waking and night time dreams. You are more likely to have a lucid, clearer perception, understanding, and response to both your lucid and non-lucid dreams.

A step-by-step process that even children can follow, IDL nevertheless accesses the transpersonal realm of the sacred. It does so by amplifying emerging perspectives that embody qualities that are components of enlightenment: confidence, empathy, wisdom, acceptance, inner peace, and witnessing. These in turn amplify your experience of core qualities of the sacred: luminosity, cosmic humor, and abundance. "Luminosity" refers to a clarity and objectivity that transcends time, space, and individual consciousness. "Cosmic humor" refers to a balance and wisdom that smiles at fear, drama, and personalization. "Abundance" is a sense of the ever-present, inherent regenerative creativity of life. IDL anchors your life in these qualities. As it does so, your ability to live your daily life free of drama increases and quality of your decisions improves. Best of all, you can easily test these claims yourself.

This text focuses on explaining IDL interviewing. However, IDL contains a number of tools for reducing filtering that blocks clarity and other tools for enhancing waking dream, deep sleep, shamanic, mystical, and near death state experiences. These are described in *Waking Up.*[1]

---

1 Dillard, Joseph *Waking Up. How to Use Integral Deep Listening to Transform Your Life.* Deep Listening Publishing, Berlin, Germany, 2014. ´

1: Awakening Your Muse

In 1816 Samuel Taylor Coleridge had a remarkable "opium dream," of the mysterious pleasure dome of Xanadu, which he proceeded to write down. It became the first section of his captivating poem, *Kubla Khan:*

> In Xanadu did Kubla Khan
> A stately pleasure-dome decree:
> Where Alph the sacred river, ran
> Through caverns measureless to man
> Down to a sunless sea.
> So twice five miles of fertile ground
> With walls and towers were girdled round:
> And there were gardens bright with sinuous rills
> Where blossomed many an incense-bearing tree;
> And here were forests ancient as the hills,
> Enfolding sunny spots of greenery.
>
> But oh! that deep romantic chasm which slanted
> Down the green hill athwart a cedarn cover!
> A savage place! as holy and enchanted
> As e'er beneath a waning moon was haunted
> By woman wailing for her demon-lover!
> And from this chasm, with ceaseless turmoil seething,
> As if this earth in fast thick pants were breathing,
> A mighty fountain momently was forced:
> Amid whose swift half-intermitted burst
> Huge fragments vaulted like rebounding hail,
> Or chaffy grain beneath the thresher's flail:
> And 'mid these dancing rocks at once and ever
> It flung up momently the sacred river.
> Five miles meandering with a mazy motion
> Through wood and dale the sacred river ran,
> Then reached the caverns measureless to man,
> And sank in tumult to a lifeless ocean:
> And 'mid this tumult Kubla heard from far
> Ancestral voices prophesying war!
> The shadow of the dome of pleasure
> Floated midway on the waves;

1

Where was heard the mingled measure
From the fountain and the caves.
It was a miracle of rare device,
A sunny pleasure-dome with caves of ice!

At this point Coleridge was interrupted by a man at his door who had some business to conduct. When he returned to his writing, he could not recapture his vision, but only write about his memories of it:

A damsel with a dulcimer
In a vision once I saw:
It was an Abyssinian maid,
And on her dulcimer she played,
Singing of Mount Abora.
Could I revive within me
Her symphony and song,
To such a deep delight 'twould win me,
That with music loud and long,
I would build that dome in air,
That sunny dome! those caves of ice!
And all who heard should see them there,
And all should cry, Beware! Beware!
His flashing eyes, his floating hair!
Weave a circle round him thrice,
And close your eyes with holy dread,
For he on honey-dew hath fed,
And drunk the milk of Paradise.

The "damsel with a dulcimer" is Coleridge's poetic muse. She personifies the creative state of mind that created the first section of his visionary poem. Because of his interruption, Coleridge lost that connection and then had to complete his poem from a waking, conscious state of mind. The result is magnificent but different from the first section, and if Coleridge had not been interrupted in his writing, we would not have had the amazing work of art that he has left us, written partially by his poetic muse and partially by his waking sense of poetic artistry. But what if Coleridge had not been interrupted? What if he had handled the interruption differently? What if the Damsel with the Dulcimer had been able to finish her poem?

Alas, we shall never know the answer, as provocative as the question may be. The best that we can do is learn from Coleridge's gift to us. This is not only the gift of his poem, but of the experience in which it is embedded – his ability to contact his poetic muse, the interruption and its consequences, and his life in general. There are so many times in our lives when we need the direction of inner

2

inspiration, creativity, and wisdom. Like Coleridge, the times when our muse speaks seem so precious and few. When we do connect, it is only for brief moments; then we lose it again. How would your life be different if you were able to access not just one, but any number of muses, depending on the task at hand? What if you had access to subjective sources of objectivity that knew you better than you know yourself? What if each were specialists in the different life areas that matter most to you and with which you most struggle? How would your life be different if, when you lost contact with your muse, you were able to reestablish contact? How could you go about accomplishing such a rare and important skill?

First, it is obvious that no muse could create such beautiful work if Coleridge had not put in long and disciplined hours mastering his craft. All of the necessary background work that led up to this epiphany is rarely considered by history. It is forgotten as we become lost in the beauty of his prose. The years of required background labor become more obvious when we consider what poetic abilities Coleridge still manages to express in the second section of *Kubla Khan* despite his failure to reconnect with his muse after his interruption.

We can see that a lifetime of preparation is spent creating a life context in which inspiration can be successfully received and transmitted. Coleridge's life practice, spiritual discipline, or *yoga,* was his writing, and for his efforts he gained access to a source of inspiration that seemed beyond him.

How might your life be different if you were able to access one or more muse for each different sort of life circumstance you face? What if you could access one personal muse to help you write, another one for conflict resolution, and another that is a specialist at making money? You would then need a life practice that was not artistically specialized like Coleridge's was. You would need one that was *integral,* because it would have to involve and integrate the various threads of your life, some of which are contradictory. Such a practice would prepare you to take advantage of the creativity and inspiration of each and every muse whenever they chose to descend. Such a practice, when it attempts to integrate all aspects of life into a congruent whole, is called an *integral life practice,* or *yoga.* Through learning to practice profound, inner listening to your own personal muses you can integrate your inner and outer worlds, your potentials and persona, and your deepest strivings with the practical demands of everyday life. This is the amazing process, called Integral Deep Listening, that you will explore in the following pages.

Regardless of the challenges you face in your life today, your muses offer perspectives that enrich your own. The Greeks recognized first three and finally nine muses of poetry, history, love poetry, music, hymns, tragedy, dance, comedy, and astronomy. From this list we realize that the Greeks not only sought inspiration for almost any pursuit, but assumed that such inspiration was accessible to all of us, regardless of the task at hand. Could it be that your personal muses are even now offering solutions to your life issues that are novel, yet practical? Are you listening? Are you in touch with your own muses as they speak to you in your dreams and through the issues of your everyday life?

People routinely come up with all sorts of reasons not to trust, much less listen to, internal sources of guidance. In over thirty-five years of encouraging such connections, I have heard countless excuses, explanations, rationalizations, and justifications that all boil down to a dismissal of one's own inner potentials. At the same time, healthy skepticism leads to committed action, if those doubts are effectively addressed. For example, it is reasonable to think, "Why would I need to distract and confuse myself by listening to a number of different internal voices?" Isn't that dissociation and fragmentation? Isn't that what psychiatrists call 'decompensation?'" Ken Wilber's pre-trans fallacy differentiates between the chaos of many prepersonal selves not yet integrated into who we are, on the one hand, and the interdependence and coexistence of many selves available to an integrated sense of self, on the other. Most of us have not accessed these inner potentials because we have not learned to discriminate between the roof-brain chatter of our monkey mind, regressed voices of inner confusion and clear, and autonomous inner voices that personify our potentials. We have not learned to differentiate among voices of external authority, the internalization of those voices as conscience or intuition, our own waking preferences, and the priorities of our own inner, or life compass. This book was written to help you make these important distinctions and put them to use in your life.

Would you like to be more connected to your own personal muses? Would you like to be able to stay in touch with them when life events conspire to separate you from them? IDL is a type of dream yoga. It is the approach to deep listening to your muses that you will explore here. A "yoga" is any discipline whose purpose is oneness with life. What most people call "yoga" is one particular type, focused on physical agility, focus, and relaxation called *hatha yoga.* *Karma yoga* uses life work to become one with life.

Jnana yoga (*Jnana* is the Sanskrit root for *Zen*) does the same with meditation. *Bhakti yoga* uses devotion to become one with life. IDL views everyday life as a self-created and culturally-maintained delusion based on lifelong habits of thinking, feeling, and social scripting. Those who practice IDL daily learn to view life as a dream of their own creation, in that how you respond to the moment is determined by how you interpret your experience. That in turn is determined by your level of development and the breadth of the perspective, world view, or context that frames your perception. While Tibetan dream yoga teaches the use of waking up within your dreams, called lucid dreaming, to learn to wake up from the dream of life, IDL makes waking up in your everyday life a priority because your waking perceptual framework is what makes sense not only of your waking, but your dream, lucid dreaming, mystical and shamanic experiences. IDL helps you awaken from your self-created life dream through interviewing dream characters and personifications of life issues that are most important to you. These characters, through the trans-rational magic of IDL, clarify and amplify your

4

emerging potentials – those characteristics and processes that life is wanting to birth into your consciousness as directive muses. IDL will show you how these interviewed emerging potentials personify liberating perspectives on the life issues that matter most to you: money, relationships, health, your spiritual path, and love. IDL will also teaches you to actively identify with and *become* perspectives that know better than you how to meet your unique life challenges successfully. Through practicing IDL, you will learn how to actively seek out the particular muses you need at this point in your life and feel them come alive within you, thereby preparing you for the descent of multiple personifications of authentic light, wisdom, and creativity.

If Coleridge had known about IDL he may have handled the knock at his door differently. Perhaps he would have decided that his muse and her transmission took precedence over the business at the door. His life priorities would have been so clear to him that events would have been far less likely to create obstacles to his highest and clearest intentions. If he had practiced IDL, Coleridge could have reconnected with the Damsel with the Dulcimer after his interruption. He could have allowed her to finish her transmission of her poem.

Phenomenology is an experimental and experiential methodology of self-examination. It requires you to recognize and set aside as many of your assumptions about yourself, others, and life as you can in order to more fully and clearly listen to what life has to say to you. IDL is a lifelong phenomenological discipline designed to prepare you to take advantage not only of those moments when the heavens open but also those times when you are cast into nightmare and outer darkness. It does so by showing you how to partner with your muses as you meet the mundane challenges of your every day life. IDL prepares you to recognize and disregard both interruptions and deviations from your highest purposes and greatest good. It can help you create your life as a work of art in a way that reflects the best that life has to offer. In this way, like Coleridge, you will be able to bequeath the world a great gift: an authentic life that evokes the best in others.

Exercises

Have you ever felt as if you were possessed by a flash of insight, a sense of life purpose, an artistic impulse that was so strong that it felt both divine and wholly "other?"

Is there one particular area in your life where such contact is stronger than in others?

Are there activities that seem to encourage the descent of your muse more than others?

Are there particular times that seem to encourage the descent of your muse more than others?

2: What is an Integral Life Practice?

Everyone that wants to heal, balance, and transform needs to have an integral life practice. Without one we grow piecemeal, living a life full of experiences but without the purpose and sense of direction that comes from an integrating core direction that infuses every aspect of our life. "Integral life practice" is a term developed by Ken Wilber and the Integral Institute of Boulder, Colorado that builds on work described by George Leonard and Michael Murphy of the Esalen Institute in their book *The Life We Are Given*. It describes the practice of personal spiritual disciplines that support the evolution of human potential. An integral life practice, or ILP, is a psychospiritual discipline built around a set of instructions. These instructions or *injunctions*, are directions that you put to the test in the laboratory of your own life.

An integral life practice is a particularly potent form of personal practice. It is a discipline, in that it requires consistent commitment to a course of action. Integral disciplines are transpersonal, in that they are designed to integrate the entirety of consciousness, including its prepersonal, personal, and transpersonal dimensions. Such practices are called *yogas,* in that they are psychospiritual disciplines designed to amplify oneness with life.

Daily practice grounds the fullness of life in the body and emphasizes healing. Healing is the elimination of internal conflict and the return of homeostasis. When this is done, positive health and vitality are experienced. This is accompanied by increased alertness, wakefulness, and empathy. Your daily practice of IDL is designed to invite in your muses. It also involves their evocation in your daily life. Your muses are members of your own internal spiritual support community, or *Sangha*. "Sangha" is a Buddhist word that means "spiritual community." As sangha members, they work for your personal healing, balancing, and transformation.

An integral practice is *dharmic*. "Dharma" is a Sanskrit word that means "action," and "universal law." It involves the expression of your authentic intentions in ways that are in alignment with life.

A *dharmic* integral life practice addresses the needs of the whole person, body, mind, and spirit, interpersonally and intrapsychically, not from the perspective of *your* personal wants and needs, but from the perspective of life's agenda for your growth. Integral practices take into account all your lines of development, including your growth in wisdom, acceptance, physical strength and coordination, ethics, empathy, and communication skills. It takes into account all four quadrants of the human holon, which include your internal and external worlds as well as your individual and collective experience. An integral practice works to heal, balance, and transform not only your waking life, but your sleeping, dreaming, and meditative states of consciousness as well. It attempts to transcend

6

gender issues by cultivating the strengths of both masculine and feminine aspects of your androgynous potential. Integral practices take into account prepersonal, personal, transpersonal, and non-dual developmental perspectives. They seek wisdom as the antidote to the suffering caused by ignorance and attachment.

An integral life practice is transformative. It awakens you, changing your relationship with others, with your body and mind, with money, with your career, and with your reasons for living. IDL teaches a central skill: deep listening to those muses that personify core qualities of life awakening within you. It is a life perspective centered in confidence, empathy, wisdom, acceptance, inner peace, and witnessing. In IDL, these characteristics inform, direct, and modify your integral life practice. Secondly, they expand your sense of self through the practice of identification with personifications of your innate, authentic potentials. As your waking agenda becomes increasingly aligned with the priorities of life you heal, balance, and transform. You attain an ability to maintain multiple stable perspectives that transcend and include more limited and confining ones.

IDL teaches you first how to contact and then how to maintain deep, fulfilling, intimate ongoing relationships with the emerging potentials portrayed in your dreams and by your waking life issues. Think of it as deeply listening to your own personal muses in order to create a powerful internal support system called your *intrasocial sangha.* This process is supported by the core practice of interviewing dream characters and personifications of your life issues in a structured way that is designed to defuse internal conflicts, speed healing and the attainment of higher order vitality and identify barriers to homeostasis while supporting integration and maintaining transformation through alignment with internal muses that personify your deepest and broadest potentials. Your muses are your teachers, and in IDL they act as vital internal consultants for every area of your life.

What does an integral daily practice look like? Students of IDL set one year, six months, one month, and one week goals in the areas of exercise, nutrition, health maintenance, communication skills and relationships, finances, and spiritual development. Those goals are then submitted to dream characters and personifications of your life issues, particularly those that score high in some or all of the core transpersonal qualities mentioned above. This is done to see if your goals are *in alignment* with the priorities of interior muses in order to do two things. First, it reduces filtering or distortion and internal conflicts that often sabotage goal attainment. Second, it expands and deepens your capacity for clarity, lucidity, wakefulness, and enlightenment. You may well find that your dream characters and personifications of your life issues emphasize different goals than you do! If so, IDL will teach you how to reconcile those two different sets of priorities.

What does IDL look like? Here is an amusing personal example, to help you get a feel for the process. I've been an expert procrastinator all my life, having the equivalent of at least a Ph.D., if not post-doctoral proficiency, in this critical life competency. This last year I've had a lot of foot-dragging around filling out the necessary forms to become certified to provide seminars in my work to various professional groups. So I sat down in front of my computer and thought of how I feel when I am procrastinating. Not good! This is an example of interviewing a life issue. In this case it is the life issue of procrastination. By thinking about how procrastination makes me feel (Not good!) I am accessing a *feeling* that is associated with the behavior (procrastination). When I had that feeling firmly in mind, I asked myself, "What color does that feeling remind me of?" *Pea Soup Green!* Ug! I then imagined the space in front of me filled with an amorphous cloud of green pea soup! Not a pleasant experience! Next, I allowed the cloud to congeal, condense, or crystallize into a shape. It became a green lizard! Now I had a character, just like a dream image, to interview! This process of first identifying a life issue, then an associated feeling, allowing that to be associated with a color, and then to watch the color take form, roughly parallels the process you follow every night in the generation of your night time dreams. You go to sleep with issues on your mind. The associated feelings take form as images in relationships in your night time dramas! Once you have identified a resonant image, it is time to see what, if anything it has to say to you. Here's how the interview went with my Yodaesque lizard!

OK, green lizard, why am I having so much resistance to filling out these forms??

How should I know? I'm just a stupid imaginary green lizard, a figment of your imagination!!!

OK, sorry. Too direct an approach. Lizard, what do you like best about yourself?

I'm fast when I decide to move. Most of the time I don't. I'm patient. I'm quite still.

Oh, I get it! I had a character like you a while back that I forgot about! I think it was in a dream! Something about focused energy! Something about not doing anything, looking lazy, but being very effective, very focused when you do act! Well, that's nice, but so what? I've got the lazy part down but not the focused action part. I will procrastinate, then when I do act, I might do part of the job only, depending on what it is! So Lizard, what don't you like about yourself?

What I don't like about myself is nothing. I don't see that I have any weaknesses. If I were in charge of your life I'd be more action oriented, less reflective, less emotional. I'm a part of you that doesn't waste a lot of energy thinking about stuff. "Do or not do – there is no try!" I'm no-nonsense because I'm real, authentic, focused, and get the job done. It makes my life so much simpler than yours!

OK, so I am hearing that you are telling me that I need to be more like you if I want to get beyond my resistance, because resistance is about that reflective, emotional stuff, and you don't do that. You are all action. Is that right?

Right! You've got it!

By doing this interview I gained a lizard partner in facing those life tasks I'd rather not do. Mostly we stay laid back, cruising through life, rather like sunning on a big rock. But when it gets time to do something that involves resistance, I become my lizard! He jumps into action, sticks out his tongue, and catches a fly! Then he's still again! This model worked for me because it gave me permission to be comfortable with my habitual, relaxed self, which is who I am some ninety percent of the time. It also changed a stressful, aversive, pressuring issue into something comic, what IDL calls "cosmic humor." Such humor looks irrational but, upon close examination, it creates meaning where there was none, in ways that make fun of drama and our sense of personal angst. This interview gave me not only an image, but *an experience* of how I could remain true to my nature and still get a lot done. This was important, because it is important that we not guilt-trip ourselves for not expressing our potentials. That's not realistic! The way I used my time became much more effective, because actions outside my comfort zone were taken decisively and surgically, with the help of my lizard muse, and were then over!

Remember that your own, personal encounter with IDL will be unique. Lizards condensing out of green pea soup may sound like a ridiculous waste of time for you, but then your unique, spontaneous solutions will probably strike others as odd or ineffective as well. To become *authentic,* you must find and use a method that continuously honors and evokes your own unique solutions to your life challenges, regardless of whether they make sense to others or whether or not they find them inappropriate. Cultural assumptions and preferences are an important part of growing up, and transcending them is an important part of transpersonal development. That's what IDL will do for you – help you find your own unique solutions to your own deepest life challenges. Any integral life practice is work. But worthwhile work can also be fun, if you approach it in the right way. Hopefully my lizard conveys some of the lighthearted nature of this powerful and transformative transpersonal practice.

As a way of developing a clearer understanding of IDL as an integral life practice, we will now explore how it came to be developed.

Exercises

What sort of life disciplines do you presently pursue?

Are they in alignment with your most authentic priorities? If you think so, how do you know?

What difference would it make in your life if your waking life was increasingly reflective of your most authentic priorities?

3: Why Do People Stay Stuck?

Joanna put her head in her hands and cried. "Why is it that no matter what I do nothing seems to change? I try so hard! But then I still end up sleeping with guys who are more messed up than I am!" Why do I keep doing this to myself? Another client, Mike, looked at me and said, "The way I stay stuck is simple. I learned early on that if I demanded the best from myself that I would be rewarded with praise and good grades. Now I'm the top doctor in my field and I can't back off and enjoy life. It's as if I'm afraid that if I stop mentally whipping myself I'll be worse than useless"

At one time or another, most of us have felt trapped by the circumstances of our lives, whether married or single, rich or poor, young or old. Then, to add insult to injury, we often become imprisoned by our habitual reactions to our circumstances, which only make them harder to bear. Some people drink from a deep well of loneliness and sadness while others continuously worry. Others spend their lives trying to avoid feeling stuck by throwing themselves into work, hobbies, relationships, or travel. Most of us anesthetize ourselves by using favorite addictions to enter an oblivious trance state, entombing ourselves in a sarcophagus of comfort.

At one time or another, most of us blame something outside of ourselves for our problems. If it isn't fate or bad genes, it's how we were raised, our government, the state of the economy, other people holding us back, or how our family mistreated us. If that doesn't work, we blame people who are "different" in nationality, politics, religion, race, or class. When these avoidance strategies don't work, we may blame ourselves. We're sinners, stupid, worthless, or we just don't have what it takes to be happy in life. Many religions and "spiritual" teachings justify blaming others, ourselves, or both with prerational and abusive doctrines like Holy War, original sin, and karma. Such beliefs are destined to become quaint mythologies, because humankind is quickly outgrowing them, as the empty churches throughout humanistic Europe and the outlawing of caste system in India, based on the doctrine of karma, attest.

People everywhere are beginning to understand that when we blame others we give away our power and control over our lives because, if others are the cause of our unhappiness, we cannot be happy unless others change. We thereby give others we fear or disrespect the power to keep us unhappy. Is that wise? As long as we insist on blaming politicians, priests, parents, teachers, bosses, or God we will end up feeling controlled by individuals and forces beyond our control. If, on the other hand, we are the cause of our own unhappiness, we can learn to be happy whenever we choose to be, regardless of who we are dealing with or what they say or do. We thereby give ourselves the power to choose who and how we will think and feel.

Similarly, people everywhere are waking up to the realization that blaming themselves is like whipping a mule to get it to go faster. At some point all you have is a beat-up, resentful, sullen, broken mule, unable to move no matter how hard you hit it. As people give up blame, they outgrow those cultural institutions that use it to maintain social control. They stop wasting time focusing on who is to blame, which is a problem-centered approach to life. Instead, they keep their attention centered on finding solutions, which empowers them and supports their development.

Rather than wasting time blaming others or themselves, people are learning to *listen.* We are starting to understand that the reason that other people don't listen to us is that we don't listen to ourselves. Do you think that you do listen to yourself? Do you know your own mind? Most people believe that they do. They think that if there is one thing that they do well, it's talking to themselves! We listen to our own self-talk all day long. Although it generally feels spontaneous, about ninety percent of what we think and feel is so habitual that it is highly predictable. We listen to the same "monkey mind chatter" day after day, assuming that it represents who we are. Does it?

Listening to our habitual self-talk is not the same as practicing deep listening to ourselves. At any one time, the internal voice you think is "you" is speaking for only a minority of the entirety of who you are. For example, when you decide to throw a fit, what part of yourself are you listening to? Does that voice represent your greater interests or some limited, but loud and insistent, internal constituency?

We usually make such choices based on our momentary desires. While it *feels* like there is just one self to listen to, that is an illusion. You are made up of many selves, and the one that you are experiencing right now as you read these words is radically different from the one that you experienced when you first woke up this morning.

The reason most of us do not really listen to ourselves is not only because we don't want to, because we are afraid of what we will discover about who we "really" are, but because we *don't know how* to deeply listen to ourselves. You have a waking sense of who you are that you have carefully built up over the years in order to adapt to your unique circumstances. You had to develop your strong sense of who you are to adapt to the rules of your family and school and to learn control. However, your normal waking point of view presents only one of many legitimate ways of seeing your life. We know this to be true because we are different people at work, at home, at school, or out having fun. When we assume different roles our sense of who we are changes, and most of the time we don't even realize it, even though there may be glaring inconsistencies between who we are at work and at home, with friends or with an employer. Together these different roles form your waking persona, or mask. The reason why you stay stuck is because you stay fixated in those habitual roles that make up your waking persona. They form a comfortable addiction, that gives you a sense of stability

11

and control, and you don't know how to break yourself out of it. One person might learn that staying angry was an effective way of dealing with the unfairness of childhood abuse while another learned that never being angry was the way to gain praise. Both people will grow up to be unprepared for life, the first alienating people unnecessarily while the second will not know how to deal with the anger in others or in themselves. Chronic identification with the many waking roles that make up who you think you are is your core addiction, of which other addictions, such as alcohol and drug addiction, codependency, sex, food, and Victimization are merely symptoms. You may be thinking, "Certainly the solution to the confusion of my many internal life roles is to develop one consistent view of the world that corresponds to what is real or practical." This is the thinking behind a unitary concept of the soul and God.

If we can just find that *one* perspective that is *real* and *true* our problems will be over! History is littered with people who were so sure that they had found the One Truth that they proceeded to foist it on everyone around them.

This is the dirty little secret: the need for One Reality and One Truth is based on fear and insecurity. Consequently, belief that there is One Reality and One Truth and that you have it generates grandiosity, arrogance and hubris.

IDL offers a counter-intuitive alternative to this basic human dysfunction. It encourages you to listen to and embrace a menagerie of internally consistent but often conflicting perspectives. How could this possibly help? How could the solution lie in the cultivation of yet *more* roles if the ones we have create endless confusion? The problem is that any one perspective is finally a limit and an illusion while the ability to shift when appropriate from adaptive role to adaptive role is a form of flexibility that creates freedom. This is exactly opposite of what we were taught as children and also by the religious traditions of the world: find *yourself*; find your one, true identity, your soul, Atman, God. To do the exact opposite sounds not only irrational but counter-intuitive, and believe me, it is a hard sell. It sounds and feels threatening to many people at prepersonal levels of development and those whose identity has gained them wealth, fame, or power. There is a time and place to build a strong sense of self – generally in the first half of life. However, many IDL interviews with children have proven that far from fragmenting or interfering with the development of a sense of self, the ability to take many perspectives is not only natural for children, but *strengthens* their confidence and self-esteem. This is because the ability to shift from perspective to perspective provides children and adults with a way to contact a sense of life that lies beneath, yet interpenetrates all possible roles, perspectives, and world views. You find and learn to live from perspectives advocated by life itself rather than from stereotyped cultural and societal roles.

IDL is an alternative to paths that put your growth in the hands of professionals, gurus, psychics, and interpreters.

It was developed in response to repeated attempts, over many years, to believe in and trust various experts, gurus, religions, and spiritual teachers. For example, a major influence in my youth, from thirteen until about twenty-one, were the psychic readings of Edgar Cayce.

This work has a great deal to recommend it, and I was very fortunate to be exposed to it at an early age, because it caused me to question most of the assumptions of the cultural and social assumptions of my childhood world view.[2] I saw how the Edgar Cayce readings, as accurate as they could be regarding the diagnosis and treatment of physical ailments, could be extraordinarily inaccurate about oil wells in Texas and Earth changes. I saw how most enlightened masters, if enough data about their personal lives was available, were shown to have serious personal flaws. I saw how many people spent their lives running from one relationship to the next, from one town to another, from one job to the next, from one teacher to the next, only in time to leave each with a sense of dissatisfaction, if not in great disillusionment.

Not only was I thoroughly convinced that my waking identity was too limited to see the "big picture" of my life, but I became very skeptical of the truth claims of others. When I spent the end of my college days at the University of Texas in Austin with friends who were also interested in the psychic readings of Edgar Cayce, I got to know a psychic I had first met on a trip to the Middle East that I took when I was thirteen. His name was Ray Stanford, and he was a remarkable man. He could lay down, go into trance, and give readings like Cayce did, only they mostly covered past lives, present circumstances, and future trends rather than physical health conditions.

In one reading Ray told me that I had been a minister in New England over a hundred years before. It must have been in the early to middle eighteen hundreds, because according to this psychic reading I had come across some of the first English translations of Hindu scriptures at that time.

According to this narrative, the truth of reincarnation struck me then, in that life as a minister, as self-evident, and in my excitement I started to do a very stupid thing: I started teaching reincarnation from the pulpit of my church. I knew the Truth and I had to convince others about it. The result was that I got literally tarred and feathered and carried out of town on a rail!

This rejection and humiliation affected me so deeply that I came into this life with a strong distrust of authority figures and an unwillingness to put myself into positions of authority over others. On some primal level, I didn't trust myself.

Now, I don't know if this actually happened or whether this story was a convenient way of explaining part of how I have tended to see the world. In any case, it was true that I was very interested in seeking reliable sources of life direction that were largely independent of cultural scripting and external authority. We all tell ourselves stories about who we are, where we came from, and where we are going. To the extent that we believe that these stories are true,

---

2 For an autobiographical explanation of the evolution in world views that led to the development of IDL, see *Three Transformative world views*, *http://integraldeeplistening.com/three-transformative-world-views/*.

they create our sense of self and largely determine the life choices that we make. This was a story that I told myself at that stage of my life, and that seemed valid and valuable. It was only much later that I came to understand that such stories are selected as valuable because they validate certain script assumptions that validate our choices and trap us in self-created predestination.[3]

IDL views limitations, deficits, accidents, health problems, relationship and career crises as wake-up calls to be listened to. Notice that most people, most of the time do not listen to what such events are telling them about what is out of balance in their lives.

They simply draw conclusions based on comfortable assumptions of long standing, such as, "I got sick (or had this life crisis) because it's my karma, I sinned and God is punishing me, I'm working too much, I haven't taken care of my health, it's fate, it's my destiny, it's God's will, God is testing me, my sickness is OK, because everything is in divine order, God is calling me home, God wants me to repent, my genes are defective, life is not fair and I have bad luck." Do any of these rationalizations sound familiar?

Rather than relying on stories, excuses, justifications, and rationalizations that we tell ourselves, IDL interviews one or more personification of some aspect of the crisis. Perhaps it is the personification of anger at getting fired or the fear of approaching death; perhaps it is an externalization of one's fear of loneliness or of failure. In this way, IDL encourages the temporary suspension of our explanations and stories in order to attempt to listen to what the crisis or nightmare itself has to tell us. We already know why we think this nightmare happened. But what about the nightmare itself? Why does *it* think it is in our lives?

When we conduct such interviews we generally find that the personification of the the nightmare or crisis itself, be it an elephant, toothbrush, angel, or cloud, views the experience as a wake-up call to be listened to. This listening consists of forming different, broader conclusions and using them to think, feel, and act differently, in ways that are healthier and balanced.

This approach has helped many people to learn to see their limitations and deficits as important allies and sources of transpersonal support. It can do the same for you. Clearly, there are many life circumstances that are out of your control and are not going to change just to make you happy. However, you can always choose how you perceive those situations. Other perspectives that you can access are not stuck like you are because they view your life from relatively autonomous and objective perspectives. As you learn to look at your world through their eyes you become unstuck. You get out of your own way. Your life starts to flow.

Getting unstuck is most fundamentally the process of disidentifying with the "you" that is stuck and becoming emerging potentials that aren't. Most people do

---

3 For how IDL views and uses life script analysis, see *Waking Up*. Deep Listening Publishing, Berlin, Germany, 2014.

not recognize that they are constantly bombarded by potentials seeking to be recognized and developed. These are as plentiful as the characters in your dreams and in the multitude of life issues that you have. Think of your emerging potentials as both sunshine and rain, basic and abundant resources that are often taken for granted and therefore not used. While you may be stuck, these emerging potentials are not stuck, wounded, confused, or fossilized.

They are like an unrecognized mine in your back yard, full of gold, diamonds, and precious jewels, sitting there while you live in relative poverty, oblivious to the riches that you can acquire at any time. The emerging potentials that you access with IDL will explain to you how your life will be enriched by amplifying them in your life.

Jane was a student of IDL who had grown children and was recovering from a recent traumatic divorce from an evangelical minister. She shared a dream that had repeated from her childhood into her late 40's. In it she was going to school on a bus and realized she had forgotten her shoes. She was very afraid that she was going to be punished by her parents for her thoughtlessness. In her IDL interview of this repetitive dream, Joy imagined that she was the school bus. It said, "Joy had this dream because she felt like she had no control over a lot of things in her life, but yet at the same time she was supposed to be responsible for everything. As a little girl, she had to be responsible. She doesn't have to be responsible for everything now as an adult, but she still feels like she does."

This was a revelation to Joy. She said, "My parents still hold me responsible as an adult for everything that goes on! The shoe issue is that if I'm not responsible, then I feel guilt and have a big feeling of irresponsibility. But when I became this school bus I realized that it's not the end of the world!" With this awareness, this dream that had been with her most of her life went away. Through IDL, Joy had accessed an emerging potential, one that embodied a new life perspective for her, in the form of an imaginary dream school bus. It embodied a perspective that provided a new, liberating way for Joy to look at her life that allowed her to stop trying to avoid the criticism of others and, more importantly, her own feelings of irresponsibility and guilt. Putting IDL to work in her life, Joy would imagine she was the school bus in those life situations where she found herself blaming herself. Because the school bus did not blame her and it was a part of her that did not blame itself, practice becoming the school bus daily allowed her to finally outgrow a lifelong addiction to critical feelings that held her back. This is the liberating power of accessing and becoming emerging potentials. They create ways of problem-solving, of seeing yourself and others, that transcend, yet include, your own.

Carrie dreamed that a teacher told her that she was blocked. Her feelings of resistance to change were like a brick that others thought needed to be moved. This is an example of a life issue that is normally viewed as an obstacle and so is a source of conflict. How could it possibly be an emerging potential? When interviewed, the brick said, "I'm as big as a boulder, too big to move. I'm made out of stone, the type that you line fireplaces with. I am in front of Carrie. My function is stop her from making a mistake by keeping her from going forward. I do my job well. I feel pretty good about myself. If I wasn't around she might get hurt. It would be my fault. I would feel guilty. I don't want to feel responsible for her getting hurt." Carrie began to see that her resistance to change was an adaptive strategy to protect her from failure. When asked what part of Carrie it most closely represented, the brick said, "I most closely personify Carrie's stubbornness. I am whole within myself. I'm pretty powerful! If Carrie felt the way I do all the time she would get what she wanted, because I am not afraid of failure and I am extremely confident. I don't care what other people do or say. I am here; they are there. If she lived her life like I do she wouldn't be so pissed off all the time. She wouldn't take things personally! The more Carrie learns about herself, the more she will succeed, but if she succeeds I am out of a job! Carrie needs me in order for her to feel safe!" All of this was like a revelation to Carrie. After taking it all in, she said, "What I heard myself say is that there is a part of me that doesn't like to move forward because it's too risky! It's better to stay home!" From this experience Carrie saw clearly how she had learned as a child that if she didn't take risks she wouldn't fail or get rejected. She saw how she had identified with a stubborn, resistant role and sense of self as an adaptational strategy. She decided to take the brick's advice and to try to become the brick in her daily life. Notice that this is counter-intuitive, since the brick personifies her resistance. However, notice that the brick itself is not stuck in needing to feel safe or taking things personally. So paradoxically, by becoming the brick Carrie both owned her resistance to change and transcended it. As she practiced becoming her brick in her daily life Carrie reported that she was less concerned about what others thought about her. Because she was less concerned about how others were affecting her life, she had more peace of mind and was less afraid of failure. Carrie's brick provides an excellent example of how accessing an emerging potential that is the personification of a waking life issue can clarify how we keep ourselves stuck, and how our resistance holds the key to our growth. It also provides an example of how quickly and easily the solution we need is at hand within our reach if we will simply access our emerging potentials to find and follow our life compass.

Louise was a beautiful middle-aged black lady who had grown up in an urban ghetto. Although she was a successful sculptor, she had a lifetime pattern of being stuck in mental self-abuse that was made worse by a head injury that occurred when a tree limb fell on her head. She related a dream in which she saw a big gob of spit on the pavement. She got some of it on her shoe, which was disgusting enough to cause her to remember the dream and to be curious about it. When she imagined that she was the spit it hardly sounded like an emerging potential! It said, "I know I bring a nasty aggravation to people! I'm ugly! I know I'm the worst thing next to human waste! I like the reaction I give people because I'm a nasty form of yuck!" The spit continued, "I've accepted who I am, so I might as well enjoy it. My life is very short and I might as well do whatever I want. I personify the part of Louise that she wants to get rid of, that she doesn't want to face up to, her insecurity, her inability to stop people from doing whatever they want to do to her, her fears. Her life issues are her insecurities, her mother, the way she allows other people to treat her, her lack of self-respect. My strengths are my ugliness, my disgustingness. That's all I have to work with. I work with what I have. What I get out of life is other people's reaction to my ugliness. If I am gross and I can't do anything about it, then I can at least benefit from the reaction of disgust I cause in others."

Louise was horrified when she realized that she felt this way about herself. She had no idea that deep down within her lurked such a judgmental, self-critical self-concept. But Louise didn't have much opportunity to beat herself up for saying such things about herself because Spit went on to give Louise some suggestions about how to get unstuck. "Regarding her life issues, her mother is negative. She's not going to help Louise at all. Louise should think of her mother less. She should not have any guilt about not thinking about her mother. I don't have guilt about anything because I'm spit. I'd have Louise live more freely and enjoy things more."

Spit provided Louise with a perspective to take when she felt guilty about not calling her elderly mother, who only criticized her. It personified a perspective that was attempting to be born within Louise that was guilt-free. This is interesting, because we usually think that it is more loving to place the needs of others before our own. However, doing so is not loving when it causes us to be abused by others. As odd as it may seem, by imagining that she was Spit, Louise learned she could accept herself for who she was and not feel guilty about it. She began putting this radical idea to the test in her life by imagining that she was Spit in life situations where she felt judged. Instead of feeling vile and repugnant as you might expect, a wonderful thing happened. Louise grew in her ability to accept herself exactly as she was, warts and all. This degree of self-acceptance was a transformational change for Louise. While one interview broadened how she viewed herself and her life, IDL is a *yoga* and an integral life practice. Louise had to read over the interview, monitor when she remembered to be Spit during her days, and note the result. This is a major reason why IDL trains coaches and teachers in the method: we all need support to keep us on track.

Clearly, becoming spit probably wouldn't work for you or me, but then we aren't Louise. She already had that potential wanting to be born into her awareness and into her life. It was exactly what she needed, tailor-made for her consciousness, because it was the product of her own spontaneous, deep inner truth.[4]

---

4 "Spit" was not some preexisting archetype latent within Louise, waiting to be discovered. How she was stuck, as well as its solution, could have been effectively personified in any number of ways. Because self-generated imagery, whether from a dream or waking visualization, tends to be a spontaneous, authentic, and highly personal

While becoming Spit is not rational, it is not irrational, because what Spit said had the ring of truth for Louise. Becoming Spit was *trans-rational.* It put Louise in touch with a potential, yet unrealized, way she could be more free, effective, and alive. How might your life be different if you were constantly in touch with your unique emerging potentials?

How might your life be different if you stepped aside and allowed unstuck parts of your life, that have aptitudes that you lack, run your life? How would your life be different if you were routinely in touch with your personal muses and listened to their practical advice about how to live your life? No one can say how emerging potentials may present themselves to you. Revelation and real growth rarely comes from an exalted deity, angel, or extraterrestrial. That is the playful, cosmically humorous, whimsical, outrageous, wonderful part of IDL. Your transformational potentials may show up in your life as a grouchy giraffe, a green snowball, a scuba-diving French poodle, or a toilet seat made out of peacock feathers. It is difficult to get too melodramatic about life, or take yourself when you are imagining that you are a potted begonia or an anteater, or find you have a guardian octopus sitting on your head.

It doesn't matter if becoming an emerging potential seems ridiculous or not. It does not matter if the character is very threatening to you, like Spit was for Louise, or nightmare monsters seem to be. Humor and serendipity, what IDL calls "cosmic humor," can give your ponderous rational side a time out. Just being able to laugh at the amazing creativity of your own inner dream life is an important part of learning not to take yourself and your daily challenges too seriously. It helps you to appreciate the absurdity of life as you outgrow your addiction to personalization When you become emerging potentials that are unstuck, you get unstuck, to the extent that you become them. This is not an intellectual understanding but an experiential awareness called a *felt shift.*[5]

While such state alterations are often indescribable, they are also undeniable. While such awakenings may seem magical and at times even mystical, it is not magic and it is not mysterious. It is very real and it is available to you right now. It does not involve an altered state of consciousness, although it accesses a different and powerfully transformative way of looking at your life. Misery is optional, and IDL puts you in touch with emerging potentials that not only are not miserable; they are positively above the fray.

In summary, IDL interviewing is a core discipline for your integral life practice. It is the art of becoming other autonomous internal perspectives that are authentically your own, yet are objective to who you are, and to then give them voice. As we have seen, they will make recommendations, which are injunctions or instructions for positive change. As you apply those that seem

expression of our unique circumstances, it is arbitrary, yet carries a deep inner resonance.

5 "Felt shift" is a term that refers to the research into the nature of focusing done by psychologist Eugine Gendlin did at the University of Chicago in the 1950's and early 1960's.

beneficial to you, IDL will prove itself to you as a powerful method of personal development. By doing so, you internalize perspectives that free your mind and broaden your viewpoint. You will gradually become unstuck from your typical waking attitudes and viewpoints while incorporating alternative world views that promote your greater healing, integration, and transformation.

Exercises

What are the main ways in your life that you have been stuck?
What strategies have you tried to get yourself unstuck?
What seems to work best for you?
How do you sabotage your efforts to get unstuck?
Do you listen to wake up calls?
How would you know if your strategies are effective or not?

4: The Trans-Rational Magic of Deep Listening

You need both the healing of your wounds and the awakening of your potentials if you are to find wholeness on your life path. There are parts of yourself that have been locked in the cellar of your mind out of fear, ignorance, or preoccupation with other interests. There they wait in gloom, abandoned and rejected, at times rattling their chains and occasionally making their way upstairs in the dark of night to haunt your mind or create turmoil in your body. What are they saying to you? Why not listen to them? Access to dream characters and personifications of your life issues that need healing frees you from dragging the dead weight of unresolved inner conflict and fear through your life.

There are other parts of yourself that personify your potentials. As personal muses, they are more competent for certain aspects of the challenge of living than you yourself are, yet you probably remain unconscious of them, cut off from the vision, inspiration, and guidance that you need. They are like mountain-top guides that can see your way ahead through the swamps of life when you cannot. Without their support your progress is slower, bogged down in muck and brush as you watch for the snakes and alligators in your life and deal with a multitude of worries and annoyances that are like pesky mosquitoes and flies. Lost in the tangle of your every day life, you may lack the mountaintop perspective that you need to see where you are and where you are headed. Because you cannot see where you are, where you are going, or the best way ahead, you take many unnecessary detours in your life path. If you are alone, relying on your own experience, you are likely to set unrealistic goals. If you are with others who are as lost as you are, you may feel more secure but you are more likely to follow their lead and spend your life fulfilling their dreams instead of your own. Perhaps you head downhill, because it's easier, even when going uphill is much shorter. How valuable would it be to have a reliable guide in such circumstances?

Different than psychotherapeutic intervention, IDL draws primarily on your own emerging potentials, to access and amplify your life compass in ways that others cannot know, regardless of their education and skills. As important as respected authorities are, your life compass knows you better than guides, ministers, gurus, and parents ever can. As a result, you are provided not only with feedback from those you respect, but with ongoing objective feedback on your progress from respected and authentic interior sources of direction as well. Different than meditation, IDL identifies, neutralizes, and integrates fixated or stuck self-aspects into your larger sense of self.

For example, why don't we have a consultation with one of those alligators that is lurking in the swamp we were just talking about? I created it, so it's part of my life dream, part of my "life swamp." What does this alligator have to say about my life, if anything? Let's start by giving it three life issues to chew on…

1) Growing IDL; making it more available to others, particularly gatekeepers who can spread it throughout their circles of influence

2) Greater self-discipline with meditation;

3) Keeping on top of the work flow, day to day!

Alligator, what do you like best about yourself?

Alligator: I'm good at what I do, which is pretty much acting dead until I need to eat, and then... ZAP! Lunchtime!

Alligator, anything you dislike about yourself?

Alligator: No. I know my place in the scheme of things, and I fulfill my dharma.

Alligator, how can you say such Buddhist things? You're just an alligator!

Alligator: Not really! I am a creation of your mind and a resident of your mental world, because you thought me up. I'm not a biological organism, even though I am a personification of some of those attributes. So my responses have the benefit of your knowledge base and reflect them, yet they are not limited to them, because I am also semi-autonomous. However, I don't always think like you do or share your preferences.

And just because you might think I am a personification of MacLean's core reptilian brain, I have thoughts and perspectives that can only exist in a neocortex!

OK, alligator! So, what part of me do you most closely personify?

Alligator: I personify a part of you with few needs, that seems passive, but is actually quite assertive, even aggressive, but only when it needs to be. When I am not eating I am mellow and at peace. I also personify a part of you that seems primitive, primal, and even cruel to you, but is in fact an overlooked capacity for both decisiveness and peace of mind. I certainly do not need healing. I'm OK just the way I am! Would that you were as good at getting your needs met as I am!

Alligator, what part of YOU do I most closely personify?

You can ground things in ways I can't, because I'm just an idea, an intention, a potential. You are the expression through which I can live and grow.

Alligator, if you could change in any way you wanted this image of a life spent tromping around in a swamp and running into you, how would you change it?

Alligator: You would keep your cell phone on so you can communicate any time you want with the spotters on the tops of surrounding mountains. They have binoculars and can see where you are and where you need to go. You can't do that yourself, down here in this swamp. You lack the objectivity and big view from a mountain top. Better than that, I would change this fantasy so you would be able to float up out of this swamp and look around to get your bearings whenever you want. Would I change it for myself? I don't really care. I'm happy. You're not disturbing me. I don't need to take a bite out of you. I've got plenty to eat out here. Besides, I doubt if you're tasty.

Alligator, how would you score yourself, 0-10 in the following areas?

Confidence: 10 What is there to be scared of? Nothing is going to eat me!

Empathy: 6 Look, I know I don't seem very empathetic. But I only eat what I need to, I don't go to war, I don't lie, I don't call people names, and I don't run guilt trips on myself. I accept myself and others for who they are.

So maybe the problem is not with me and my behavior but with how you judge empathy.

Wisdom: 10 Do you have YOUR life figured out as well as I have mine? I doubt it.

Acceptance: 10 What is there not to accept?

Inner peace: 10 I don't worry. I am not stressed out. I am in balance with my environment and my reality.

Witnessing: 10 I see what I need to see, and that is a lot more than any actual alligator, because I possess your degree of witnessing, since you are a part of me.

If you scored like I do on an ongoing basis, nothing would bother you. You'd be focused, effective, and grow a lot faster.

How would you handle my life issues if you were me, alligator?

Well, regarding IDL, you are on track. I really can't think of anything else additional for you to do right now. Well, yeah. You could bite the bullet and finish those applications for offering continuing education units to counseling, MSW, and bodywork licensing bodies. You could also get your own CEUs (Continuing Education Credits) out of the way so that won't be nagging at you like mosquitoes in this swamp, pulling your focus away from your goals!

Regarding being more self-disciplined during meditation, the place to start with improvement is to make more time in your day. I suggest a consistent 5:00 awakening. That's what *I* do!

Regarding the work flow, be like me when you work. Be relaxed until it's time to focus. Then act aggressively in bite-sized bits. Then be relaxed again!

OK, Alligator! So here's what I'm hearing you suggest. I will put you to the test to see if you are a credible alligator by doing the following:

1) Not worrying about whether or not I am on track with developing IDL. I'll take your word for now and suspend my worries, at your suggestion.

2) Finish those CEU applications.

3) Get my own CEUs out of the way this week.

4) Get up at 5:00 every day to meditate.

5) Focus when I work, but not try to take on too much at a time. Relax between intense work periods.

6) To hold myself accountable, I will report back to you every day for a month, Alligator, on how I do with these goals.

This example illustrates how you can take any silly image[6] and use it with IDL to

----

6 Many people have a hard time understanding why listening to a toad, a brick, or an alligator would be better than listening to an angel, deceased aunt Mildred, or God. The only reason this issue arises is because we have to learn to set aside our very strong biases

clarify practical and concrete life changes that are not based on someone else's view of what you need to do next to grow. Each image, whether it arises from your waking or dreaming life, is that of one particular emerging potential, a facet in the diamond of life.

However, this alligator is not God, although he is a muse of sorts! There is no claim that he knows better for me than I know for myself. When you do an interview, you get to decide what is reasonable and helpful in what your dream characters and personifications of your life issues suggest, and what to ignore as impractical, harmful, or you are simply not awake enough to appreciate.

This interview also illustrates how badly off the mark waking interpretations can be about what an interviewed character will say. Did you expect an alligator to say such things? I didn't, although it all makes sense in retrospect. In IDL such assumptions are best suspended, in an attempt to try respectful deep listening for a change. This is why IDL is a phenomenological methodology.

There are several ways to test IDL for yourself. When you interview dream characters and personifications of your life issues and attempt to apply reasonable recommendations in your daily life, are you able to live your life in a broader, more inclusive way? Are you more accepting of yourself and others? Are there measurable personal behavioral improvements? For example, are you meditating more or better? Are you eating better? Is your work performance improved? Is your exercise routine finally paying off? Are your interpersonal relationships better? Is your relationship with your work, personal, and natural environment improved? How so?

Exercises

You may want to try interviewing some character that is a metaphorical depiction of one of your life issues, as I just did. If you do, use the questions at the end of this text. We will be discussing other uses of interviewing life issues below.

---

about what is true and what is real if we are to open to life in all its forms and to transformational sources of guidance and inspiration.

5: Your Roles, Muses, and Astonishing Potentials

There is a knock on St. Peter's door. He looks out and a man is standing there. St. Peter is about to begin his interview when the man disappears. A short time later there's another knock. St. Peter gets the door, sees the man, opens his mouth to speak, and the man disappears once again.

"Hey, are you playing games with me?" St. Peter calls after him.

"No," the man's distant voice replies anxiously. "They're trying to resuscitate me."

Our waking roles appear and disappear as we go through our day, making our chameleon changes from worker to consumer to family member so common that we scarcely notice them. Yet there is something extraordinary and magical about this simple business that we call roles. It is neither the invention of Greek thespians nor of 20th century psychologists, but an amazing evolving capacity of homo sapiens. Pretending or modeling is the work of early childhood, as explored in the social learning approach to development of Albert Bandura, particularly in his famous Bobo doll experiment.[7] In early childhood, every child imagines that they are their parent or teacher or hero. Beyond this, they imitate the behaviors they find modeled by those around them. The acquisition of language is perhaps the most common and notable example of this. Role playing is a major component of how behaviors, with their associated thoughts and feelings, that are necessary for family life and social existence are learned. In its more sophisticated form of consciously taking on another identity, such as actors do, role-playing has probably been a more recent addition to the human behavioral repertoire.

The self that we know, the self that we identify with, represents only a small range of the roles that are available to us. If we were rainbows, we would only be aware of a few of our colors. If we were water, we would be largely unaware of our potentials as ice and gas. As a result, we plan our lives and take action based on a limited set of understandings and expectations.

Consequently, how can our results be other than partial, confusing and misleading, draining us of precious resources of time and energy?

Taking the role of another allows us to perform two amazing acts at once, acts that are essential to human development. When Jane "became" School Bus she switched perspectives; she looked at life from another point of view. Relatively speaking, she "got out" of herself. She disidentified with her normal, typical point of view and identified with another perspective that was relatively free and

---

7 A "Bobo Doll" is an inflatable toy about the size of a ten year old child. Will a child exposed to examples of aggression likely be more aggressive toward the doll? Will a child exposed to examples of non-aggression likely be less aggressive toward the doll? The answer is "yes."

unstuck.

Each role you take has a particular orientation to time. Roles are either retrospective, objective, or prospective. *Retrospective* roles provide you with a different way of looking at where you have been than the perspective you normally take. They may allow you to regress to an earlier way of approaching life that may be less mature, childlike, or simply childish. For example, sports and games allow us to play again and feel some of the feelings that are permissible in childhood but less so in adults. Becoming your "inner child" is to take on a retrospective role.

Fixations are parts of ourselves that are stuck at some earlier level of functioning. Like the character Spit, which was a wounded part of Louise, part of your capacity to live fully is unavailable to you because you reject that woundedness out of fear that is who you really are. In IDL you show wounded perspectives deep respect simply by the act of becoming them. When you take the next step and actually listen to what these angry or scared perspectives have to say, you are validating the world views of those internal perspectives. Whether you agree with them or not is an entirely different matter. Through this self-validation you defuse deep-seated, long-festering internal conflicts that block your healing and your development. This frees up retrospective roles, such as Spit. It makes available to you those facets of your life force that they personify, such as Spit's self-acceptance, which was far greater than Louise's. This is why the resolution of childhood fixations in IDL is generally accompanied by a powerful sense of expansion and capability. The function of retrospective role playing is primarily therapeutic in that it allows you to heal by recognizing, acknowledging, and re-integrating broken off, forgotten, or wounded parts of yourself that you need if you are to move ahead as a whole person. This is known generally as "shadow work," and such approaches typically consider these regressive and fixated roles to be self-aspects.

Jackie, an intelligent and attractive student of IDL, had a repetitive nightmare since childhood in which her white bathroom turned lime green when she looked in the mirror. This scared her so much that she always ran away, but as she ran out of her house the hallways and rooms behind her would turn lime green too. This was very scary to Jackie. If this were your dream, what would you think created it? Here is what Jackie's bathroom had to say to her.

"I personify Jackie's emotions. She was not allowed to express them as a child. Life felt stark, like the white bathroom. All the time she was flooded with emotions, which scared her, because they were against the rules." By being the lime green bathroom Jackie could own her fear of her emotions in a healthy, balanced way that did not overwhelm her. She could give herself permission to integrate into her waking persona an important aspect of her being that she had repressed as a young child and to move beyond a lifelong fear of her feelings. Furthermore, Jackie knew exactly what it felt like to evoke that missing piece of herself, because she felt it every time she became the lime-green bathroom.

Most of us spend our lives constantly juggling many responsibilities, roles, and tasks, trying hard not to drop any of them. Your *objective* roles provide you with alternative perspectives on who you are today in your life. They show you what to emphasize in order to bring your roles as worker, student, consumer, friend, lover, and spiritual seeker into balance. They can teach you to be less passive and more assertive, less the Rescuer and more the helper. This function is primarily integrative, heterarchical, and what Wilber calls "translative," in contrast to transformative, hierarchical and transpersonal, in that it allows you to create a stable, secure, and balanced sense of who you are. Think of the importance of having a broad, stable foundation for development. For example, how high a pyramid can be built depends on the width and stability of its foundation. How high a rocket can fly depends on the strength of its launching pad and the power of its engines. Objective roles bring integration by balancing important lines of development. Examples of such lines include your cognitive, emotional, and ethical competencies, your sense of who you are, your capacity to form and manage relationships, and your capacity for empathy.

Mick, a young, handsome lawyer, was very self-critical and always pushed himself to be the best. He dreamed that he was robbing a bank with his sister. If you had such a dream, what would you think it was about? When Mick imagined that he was the money that was stolen, it said, "If I were in charge of Micks's life I would make him slow down. He needs to see the value of slowing down. I don't care about pushing; I just exist. I have value. Mick doesn't need to prove or accomplish anything. He needs to put less energy into the outcome of things and just be, like money. I don't care about the outcome of things, yet I have value, in and of myself." These comments not only helped Mick to be less self-critical but to balance his work life, since he stopped putting such intense pressure on himself to succeed by external standards. He found that he actually accomplished more. He started doing things because he wanted to do them, not because he was continuously creating internal pressure out of a need to compete with others.

Another student, Vicky, told the following dream: "I am looking at a bunch of washing machines with front glass doors, all of them with women's heads in them that are alive! There is no water in the machines but the heads are tumbling. One head is wearing really red lipstick. I think she wants to say something to me, but I wake up." Again, if you had such a dream, what do you think it might mean?

Vicki chose to talk to the head. It said, "I'm not real. My body's not real. If I could change this dream, I would stop spinning and be more stable. I want to be a head without a body. If I could change the way Vicky lives her waking life, I would improve her ability to think. I am confused, the washing machines are confused, and this bar I am in is confused."

When we talked to the red lipstick it said, "Vicky needs to be around people who she can trust.

She needs to stop being a stripper and get a regular job so that her life will be stable and she will be able to get her thirteen-year-old son back, who is in foster care." Vicky was amazed at what she heard. She stated that she had a habit of dissociating from her body as a stripper. She felt that her body had gotten her into a lot of trouble in her life and she wanted to live in her head. From this experience Vicky also learned that she dealt with her boredom by diving into relationships with men.

Vicky stopped dancing, opened a diner, and is presently working on developing a healthy relationship with her son.

Vicky's IDL interview introduced her to a new perspective on her life that not only made sense to her, but was practical and achievable.

As with Vicky, whatever is out of balance in your life surfaces when you practice IDL interviewing. This is because your dreams and life issues will act as an early warning system if you want them to. Whatever comes up, whether it is a broken relationship, disease, or death is there to help you wake up. IDL interviewing is a powerful and effective way of accessing the help that you need in order to regain balance and reintegrate different parts of yourself into a smoothly functioning whole.

Do you ever get the feeling that you really are much more capable than you usually are, but that you just don't know how to be that person? *Prospective* roles open you to your emerging potentials, to experiencing yourself as the person you can become. These potentials may seem like distant fantasies to you, but they are here and now realities or they would not be showing up in your dreams and interviews. The only reason why they are not operating in your waking life right now is because you do not own them. Because your present personality is limited and ignores or disowns perspectives that are not retrospective or personal, most prospective roles get attention. Those that do are usually life-script-based fantasies of our waking identity, like becoming a millionaire, a rock or sports star, finding one's soul mate, or traveling to exotic places. Authentic prospective roles, unlike most of these self-centric fantasies, are fundamentally transformative, in that they open up new ways of looking at yourself that are not only broader, but relatively selfless.

When Jane became the school bus in her dream she also became an emerging potential that did not see her as irresponsible and did not need her to live up to its expectations. The potential for her to "become" the school bus had been there all her life, an unrecognized internal potential, just waiting to be acknowledged. However, Jane had been out of touch with her ability to detach from both her own and other's expectations of her. This is also an example of how a retrospective role is generally transformed into a prospective one by IDL:

How many of life's challenges are you trying to shoulder? Perhaps you are playing Atlas, like Jane, taking the world on your shoulders when you could instead be getting in touch with other, unrecognized perspectives that have the outlook and skills that you lack. Paradoxically, letting go and expanding allows more competent perspectives to step forward and pick up the burden. Only for them, it's no burden at all!

As we have seen from the examples of the pyramid and rocket, transformation without integration is unsustainable. State access without grounding and application simply becomes either an addictive avoidance or a curse, like people who take psilocybin regularly but instead of expanding become jaded, chasing the next high. Have you ever gone to an inspirational workshop and felt your life open up, only to find yourself in the following days falling back in disillusionment into your old habits? What happened? You could not sustain your opening because your habitual level of comfort won out. This is why most of us must spend the vast majority of our time working to achieve the daily balance that integration requires. If we do not, we cannot sustain transformation. Instead, we fall back into our comfort zone. We lack the foundation to sustain our peak experience, our vertical opening. This is why you need an integral life practice. IDL is a yoga designed to direct and coordinate the integral life practices that you choose.

Just like we require integration of our objective roles to maintain the transformation provided by our prospective roles, integration without healing of our retrospective roles is partial at best. If you are in emotional or physical pain, that distress is going to demand your attention, impeding your ability to balance your life until you listen to it. Issues that require healing tend to emerge first and most frequently until they are heard and addressed, like Louise's Spit. They are generally the loudest voices vying for your attention. Nightmares and repetitive dreams are often expressions of unresolved retrospective roles that need healing.

All three of these types of roles, retrospective, personal, and prospective, are often discovered within the same interviewed emerging potential, as we can see in Alligator, Spit, Brick, School Bus and Vicki's Tumbling Head. This reminds us that our assumptions about what a dream character or another person represents, are usually wrong and always severely limited. Every experience in life, no matter how mundane or painful, is ideally approached not only as a wake-up call, but as a worm-hole directly into the sacred.

A second trans-rational, magical aspect of taking roles involves the act of laying down or surrendering your waking day-to-day perspective. This simple act is a statement of detachment and witnessing, both of which are core elements of transpersonal development that are also intrinsic to the human growth process. It shows up at all levels of development as the *synthesis,* or transformational stage of any dialectical growth process.[8] When a baby experiences separation from its

---

8 Originating in Fichte and amplified by many others, including Wilber, the developmental dialectic consists of three stages, thesis, antithesis, and synthesis. The thesis stage largely involves integrative, heterarchical, stabilizing and communal processes and is associated with objective roles. The antithetical stage largely involves dissociative, regressive, disruptive, and nightmarish processes and is associated with retrospective roles. The dialectic generally assumes that most of our time is spent in the thesis stage, trying to integrate our lives and maintain stability as we cope with new people, experiences, and tasks. When too much dissonance exists between our objective and our

mother or an adolescent puts distance between his values and those of his family, this fundamental growth process is occurring. Letting go of who you think you are creates the detachment and witnessing necessary for the acquisition of a broader and deeper sense of self.

Your ability to accept and use a multitude of different perspectives is a measure of your emotional and mental maturity. Past a certain fundamental level of development, taking the perspective of another requires empathy. Empathy is not only the ability to understand another person's feelings, concerns, or difficulties; it is the ability to identify with their perspective. It indicates both a willingness and an ability to surrender the safety and security of a habitual and comfortable sense of who you are in order to look at life as it appears from the circumstances of someone, or in the case of IDL, something else. Taking the role of another does not have to be limited to other humans, although we often think of it in those terms. As we have seen in the examples above, you can have empathy with the spontaneity and suffering of animals; you can identify with trees, rocks, and stardust. This greatly expands our definitions of sentience and reality. Normal categories of sacred and profane, reality and fantasy and objectivity and subjectivity no longer apply.

Young children lack empathy. They are unable to take the perspective of the bugs and animals they hurt or the other children they taunt. Normally, as children mature, they develop the ability to consider multiple perspectives, which means that they have a versatility and adaptability absent in those who do not. However, this process typically diminishes when we develop a strong unitary sense of self. We may see many perspectives in the world around us, but our own perspective remains stable and stationary. This is a core problem for humanity, because most wars and interpersonal conflicts are waged to defend one or another totally arbitrary and finally delusional perspective. When you insist on looking at your world from the perspective of your stuck self, regardless of how spiritualized it becomes, you will stay stuck, guaranteed![9] However, when you look at your world from the perspective of emerging potentials that are not stuck, you will no longer feel stuck. IDL is rather like coming home to a sense of who you authentically are.[10]

---

retrospective roles exists, wake-up calls often take the form of dream and waking nightmares. The transformation of the synthesis stage naturally occurs when proper attention is given to deep listening to retrospective, antithetical stage roles and their integration into our objective roles, or the thesis stage of our developmental dialectic.

9 As noted above, a review of the actual lives of "enlightened" personalities is a sobering experience. For example, see Falk, Geoffrey D. *Stripping the Gurus.* Million Monkeys Press, 2009.

10 The transpersonal community has a saying, "You have to be somebody before you can be nobody," (Jack Engler) meaning that you have to develop a strong, competent, centralized sense of self before you can successfully outgrow it. Consequently, I am not arguing against having a strong sense of self. Much of what I have done as a practicing

Imagine that you are the air that you are breathing right now. To do so, you must first be willing to disidentify with "yourself.". Now simply imagine that you are experiencing life as the air being taken in through your nostrils, filling your lungs, and being pumped throughout your body as oxygen, feeding your cells. Questions can help you get into the role of air. You might ask, "Air, are you fresh or stale?" "Do you like yourself, dislike yourself, or do you not care, air?" "How do you feel about this person breathing you while they are reading this book, air?" "Do you like them? Dislike them? Not care?" Such questions not only serve the purpose of putting you into the role of air, but of amplifying or expanding your awareness of what it means to examine your life from air's perspective. The result is often a view of your life that is not only different from your own, but both freeing and broadening, because you are identifying with an immediately present but prospective role. You are becoming more than you were. Once your identity expands, as it will if you really allow yourself to take on the perspective personified by air, it can never quite shrink back to the same size that it was before. This is the trans-rational magic of taking on roles and the perspectives they personify. Doing so not only expands your identity but thins it. You become less identified with who you think you are. Every time that you interview an emerging potential, you let go of your stuck, complacent self, just for a little while, and allow your sense of who you are to expand to incorporate a new, relatively free and objective perspective on your life. The more that you do so, the quicker you heal, balance, and transform. Therefore, if you want to outgrow your identification with your limited sense of self, one fundamental and powerful tool for doing so is to learn to imagine you are some other, relatively detached perspective, in a therapeutic, transformative way.

We know that people who cannot take the role of another person lack the ability to empathize. People who cannot empathize have important limits on how they can grow. This is why an inability to empathize is one possible diagnostic indicator of a personality disorder and why the expansion of one's capacity to empathize is a core developmental competency. It is also a reason why learning to take on roles is an effective therapeutic intervention not only for personality disorders but for problems at each and every stage of the developmental spiral. Even the Buddha practiced *upaya*, a Sanskrit work translated as "cunning benevolence" or "skill in means." Essentially, it is the willingness and the ability to masquerade in limited and conditioned form in order to bring enlightenment to man. In Christian mythology, this is what God does by incarnating the Christ consciousness as one man, Jesus, at one particular historical moment. God takes the role of Jesus in first century A.D. Palestine. Buddha takes the role of Gautama in sixth century B.C. India. What is this but disidentifying with one's normal identity and identifying with another role? Is that not an empathetic act?

---

therapist over the years is help people develop such a sense of self, in the full knowledge that if growth is to continue, they will someday outgrow it.

Just as you need empathy to identify with the feelings of others or the air that you breathe, you need empathy to deeply take on the transformative perspectives you need to propel your growth. Since we project our meanings onto everything that we experience, what you see in all people and all things is dependent on your awareness. The more empathy that you possess, the more accurate your projections will be. As Immanuel Kant, the 18th century German philosopher would say, your perception is conditioned by the categories of your experience. Therefore, it really doesn't matter if you imagine that you are a dream moon, an imagined moon, or a real physical moon, in that all are personifications of an innate and relatively stable set of characteristics that you associate with the moon and project onto it. All life can then be experienced as both a dream and real, at the same time. This is why IDL deals with all aspects of our experience and not merely our nighttime dreams. From the perspective of life, there is no distinction between dream lucidity and waking lucidity. It is why learning to be awake *while you are awake* is a dream yoga, and why IDL emphasizes the level of development in which dream lucidity occurs.

When you empathize with another perspective, whether it is that of another person, a dream character, or the personification of a life issue, you are performing a fundamental and powerful act of acceptance. For example, if you imagine that you are a rock, you must first get over your bias that rocks, being inanimate objects, could not possibly have anything useful to say to you. If you imagine that you are a tarantula, you must first suspend your fear of spiders. If you imagine that you are a rapist, you must first put to the side your disgust toward such depraved behavior and your revulsion toward abusers. If you imagine that you are a possessing demon, you must first overcome your fear that by doing so you will become possessed! Consequently, the very act of identification is an act not only of acceptance but also of courage. You are in effect saying, "I am strong enough to let go of who I usually think I am and who I usually feel I need to be so that I can become what life wants to make of me"

Exercises

While you can probably name all your social roles, consider all the different roles that you play in your dreams. What does it mean that they are basically unlimited in form and variety?

31

6: Common concerns about IDL

As Ken Wilber points out in *Integral Spirituality,* healthy skepticism is an important aspect of development. Skepticism and doubt are fundamental to a questioning attitude that allows you to consider new ideas and grow into new perspectives. It is a signature characteristic of the rational, or mid-personal stage of human development. Without doubt and skepticism, you will never develop beyond a simply and naive faith in what your family, teachers, and culture scripted you to accept as real and true. Consequently, IDL invites skepticism, and if you pursue this method you will encounter plenty of it. This chapter is intended to arm you with responses to some of the common doubts that people have about IDL.

How can one know that interviewed emerging potentials are the voices of your life compass? How can anyone be sure that they aren't demonic influences that are trying to trick them? How can one know that IDL is not simply some sort of preconscious ego trip designed to inflate one's self-worth by creating some delusional fantasy world? Such questions and such doubts are healthy if they aren't simply excuses to stay ignorant. If not, they will cause people you meet who learn about IDL to carefully test the process so as not over-commit themselves to a path that has not yet proven itself to them. I highly recommend such a cautious, questioning approach to any and all services, techniques, and methods that you encounter.

It is not unusual for newcomers to IDL to think, "These people doing these interviews aren't telling themselves anything that they don't already know." The answer to this concern is, "Of course! These perspectives reflect parts of them!" On some level everyone is already fully aware of the validity of what their dream characters and personifications of their life issues have to say to them. However, the truth is that this concern misses the larger issue.

Interviewed perspectives not only *include* the perspectives, and therefore the thinking, language, and emotions you know as your own, but *transcend* them, in that they contribute the thinking, language, and emotions that are unique to a cactus, star or toothbrush.

In addition, IDL works by allowing you to compare your waking priorities with those of various other relevant perspectives. Most of the time these other priorities are already known but are valued differently. For example, the lady with the nightmare of her green bathroom had always valued suppressing her emotions above giving herself permission to feel them, because her perception was that to express her feelings meant she would be criticized, ignored, or rejected. When she took a perspective that did not make that assumption, she created space to rethink her priorities. This is important; if your priorities and those of your life compass are different there will be internal conflict. What you believe you need is incompatible with what is attempting to be born into your life. The more out of alignment your waking priorities are with those of your life compass, the louder and longer lasting the wake-up call is likely to be. It is not that you do not know about these other priorities; it is that you do not emphasize them, often because you lack permission to do so.

Skepticism toward IDL interviewing is indicated by the thought, "That's just me making up these answers!" If someone raises this concern, point out to them that if that is the case, then they should be able to predict what their different dream characters and personifications of their life issues will say. If they cannot, wouldn't that demonstrate that they aren't making up at least parts of some answers? If they are not making up answers, what does that imply? Isn't the most parsimonious and likely explanation that authentic, unique, and autonomous perspectives are being expressed?

Another common doubt about the method that people may experience is, "Why should I talk to inconsequential, trivial, mundane objects in my dreams, or purely imaginary images, like meat grinders or bathroom mirrors?

Why should I assume that they might have anything of any significance to say?" IDL does not ask students to assume that the images they interview have any significance. Instead, it asks them to lay aside for the moment their doubts, expectations and beliefs, both positive and negative. Simply suspend judgment, get into role, follow the questioning process, and stay in role. Speak from the perspective of the image that is being interviewed to the best of one's ability.

There are many possible theories about how IDL works. For example, you may conclude, "Subjects are mostly getting in touch with their own fears, hopes, and dreams for their lives." While this is generally correct, it is much more than that. They are often getting in touch with *conflicting* fears, hopes, and dreams. The purpose of IDL interviewing is not simply to access different perspectives so as to heighten awareness and grow lucidity; it is to move on into applying those recommendations that are reasonable and hold promise.

Another, more direct and persuasive way of answering such doubts is to have the skeptic interview some dream character or personification of a life issue important to them. Are they willing to get into role? If not, they have no basis on which to criticize the method because they have not experienced it. If they are willing to get into role the characters themselves can be asked about their doubts and skepticisms. How do they answer? "Are the priorities of interviewed characters the same as mine?" If not, why not? If the answers in interviews are simply expressions of one's waking self, wouldn't the priorities be the same? If they are different, doesn't that imply that perspectives are being expressed that are not just your own wishful thinking? When you follow the waking life recommendations of those interviewed emerging potentials that score higher than you do in the core qualities of confidence, empathy, wisdom, acceptance, inner peace, and witnessing, what happens? Is your life improved in the areas that they predicted, or not?

IDL does not assume that the perspectives that you interview are *only* parts of yourself.

In answer to the question, "What part of the subject do you most closely personify," the image may respond that it does indeed personify this or that aspect of you or it may say something like, "I am your great aunt Matilda. I am not an aspect of you!" It may also say, "I personify your desire for nurturance in your life in addition to actually being your great aunt Matilda." In any case, suspend your disbelief about the truth of the answer and judge it pragmatically: are there recommendations that, when followed, bring transformation, balance, or healing?

IDL improves decision-making. Are not those decisions you make that take into account the perspectives of your interviewed emerging potentials more informed, broad, and objective than those that do not? This hardly means that you need to do an interview before making any decision! As you do more interviews your confidence in your judgment will probably naturally improve, particularly since you now know you have a methodology at hand to test the wisdom of your decisions whenever you think it might be helpful. In addition, most interviewed emerging potentials seem to care very little about much of what we do in our daily lives. They are not nursemaids, hall monitors, police, or priests in confession. Assume that you are on track in those areas of your life that your interviewed dream characters are not concerned about. However, if you are concerned about some issue and they are not, you can always ask them why not. Regarding those areas about which they voice opinions, take their perspectives into consideration, but remember that these viewpoints exist to inform your choices; only *you* have executive power and responsibility to make decisions for the entirety of yourself.

After all, these characters aren't Rhodes scholars or bodhisattvas. They have their areas of expertise, but most have their areas of incompetency too, so don't go putting them on pedestals, especially the dream telephone poles and toilets!

Some people feel threatened when they consider imagining that they are some other role. They wonder, "Won't this be confusing?" "Won't I fragment my personality?"

"Maybe I'll have a meltdown and turn into a gelatinous glob of protoplasm unfit for anything!" While it can be a lot of fun to scare ourselves, the truth is that these issues rarely arise with IDL, and when they do they are easily defused. You already know that by identifying with other invested perspectives you actually expand your sense of self to include and incorporate the characteristics they personify. Your perspective broadens rather than narrows. You become more integrated, not fragmented. However, people new to IDL or professionals who have a vested interest in some other approach will express doubts and skepticism not as part of a learning process but to protect themselves from investing time and energy in learning the method. Do not spend any time trying to convince such people; just focus on what works for you. As your life becomes more harmonious and you grow in confidence, empathy, wisdom, acceptance, inner peace and witnessing, people will notice.

Some of them will want what you have. They will want to know your "secret." You do not have to claim that you have access to special knowledge or that IDL is infallible. People already know that a lot of their dream characters are mundane or nightmarish and that their fantasy images lack reality. What will be new to them is the idea that such sources may prove much more valuable to them than they expect. Trying to explain this to people often encounters intellectual barriers, including very rational concerns. Because IDL is trans-rational it can easily be dismissed as *irrational* by those who cannot distinguish between the two, and that is almost everyone.

You can explain that they will encounter wounded and immature perspectives and retrospective roles that need healing. As mentioned above, these are the fixated perspectives of retrospective roles. They may express anger, fear, sadness, insecurity, loneliness, guilt, confusion, and ignorance. Other internal voices merely will mirror their own waking perspectives.

But a significant number, too many to be ignored or discounted, will personify qualities that can fairly be called unrecognized potentials embodied by prospective roles.

They are often directly and immediately experienced during interviewing as transcending one's self-definition similar to the way sunlight and rain transcend earth and flowers. It is not that they are "better" than earth or flowers, only that they hold, in relation to them, *the potential for them to become more than they are.*

Those that do pursue IDL may do so because they recognize that many interviewed emerging potentials embody characteristics that they respect and want more of: freedom from fear, peace of mind in the midst of an engaged life, empathy that heals lives, wisdom that is generous and warm, acceptance without resignation or passivity, and the objectivity that is necessary for healthy decision-making. Such characteristics are not ego based, yet they evolve out of a strongly developed sense of self in the world. They do not embody where you have been but rather who you may potentially become.

Another doubt about IDL interviewing that you may hear is, "Who I am authentically changes over time. So how can IDL put me in touch with my life compass?" The answer is that what is authentic for you is constantly changing based on your perspective at the moment and how you are growing.

There is no one static definition of "truth," "goodness," "love," or "harmony" for you to discover. No matter how wise and loving you become you will find that there are always emerging potentials being born within you, calling you to the next stage of balance and transformation.

Be aware that while most of the doubts you will encounter will be superficially based on reason, beneath them often lie well hidden emotional resistances. IDL respects and dialogues with these resistances, turning the feeling of resistance into a color and then letting it congeal into a shape. For example, to my right as I type, on my desk there is a pile of bills. Behind me on a shelf is a pile of paperwork that I know I need to address but have not. If I were to give that resistance a color, what would it be?

The color blue comes to mind. When I fill the room with it now as I type and watch it congeal, it turns into a white egg that is hovering over my right shoulder in the center of the room.

Why take the time and energy to interview a clearly imaginary white egg? Because it personifies an important part of my resistance to growth. Here's how that interview spontaneously evolves:

Egg, what are you doing floating in my room? Are you the personification of my resistance to doing my paperwork?

Nope. I'm just an egg. I have just as much a right to float here as you do to sit there.

My, you are an outspoken egg. But aren't you a figment of my imagination?

If you want to discount me by assuming that I'm not real, that's OK with me. It's your loss.

OK, Egg, what do you like most about yourself?

I like that I'm full of potential and I'm here in your life. Oh. And also, that you are paying attention to me.

Egg, I assume the potential you're full of is a chick of some sort that can hatch out of you. Is that right?

That's right!

So Egg, can we fast-forward to when the chick hatches?

Sure! A chick hatches and grows into a rooster that is pecking all over the room and leaving feathers and poop around!

Rooster! You're making a mess of my office!

Don't you know roosters don't belong in offices? Put me outside!

But if I put you out my back door, won't Mingus and Salem (dogs) try to catch you and eat you?

No, silly! They can't eat an imaginary chicken!

So rooster, now that you're outside, do you have anything to tell me about my resistance to doing my billing and paperwork?

Why are you asking me? I don't do paperwork! I live fully in the now!

If I lived fully in the now like you, would I be able to do my paperwork with less procrastination?

Who knows? Why don't you try and see for yourself!

Rooster, how do you score yourself 0-10 on the following qualities:

Confidence – 10; *Empathy* – 0; *Wisdom* – 0; *acceptance* – 10; *peace of mind* – 10; *witnessing* – 0.

Rooster, do you have resistance to anything?

Nope!

My, rooster, you are a study in contrasts! You are very strong in half of these qualities and are not in the slightest concerned with the other three. How come?

Hey – did I say I was perfect?

If you ran my life and had my waking responsibilities, how would you handle my resistance to paperwork?

I would do it immediately to get it out of my life as quickly as possible so I could do important and valuable things, like pecking and crowing!

Perhaps your confidence, acceptance, and peace of mind are the qualities that I need to overcome my resistance to paperwork. I will attempt to be you when I think about it and see if it helps me grow out of my resistance and get it done. Thanks, Rooster.

You're welcome!

So now I have a new Sangha member, a new muse who definitely has his weak areas. Clearly, I am not to rely upon him for everything. But if he is of any help at all in me getting my paperwork done quicker, that would be a great service. (Since I wrote this, months and years have passed. I am no longer much of a procrastinator. How much credit belongs to this rooster, or that alligator that was interviewed?

Honestly, I can't tell you. What I can tell you is that a life-long resistance that got me into a lot of trouble is no more, and the perspective of this rooster is something I have internalized that has definitely worked for me.)

Often my students will ask me questions like, "Why a rooster? Why not a hen or a nightingale?" I generally refer these questions to the rooster or whatever character is present at the moment. They are in a much better position to answer such questions than I am. My answers are pure conjecture.

Notice that this interview did not follow either of the interviewing protocols at the end of this text. There are very good reasons for those questions and the order in which they are presented, worked out over decades. I recommend that like a musician you develop your confidence in your ability to play scales, note read, and play standards before you launch off into the wild world of improvisation.

One of the texts in the IDL Certificate Program, *IDL Interviewing Techniques*, explains the rationale for each of the questions, their order, and issues that may come up when they are asked.

Exercises

What are your doubts about IDL and its effectiveness?

How can you get answers to those questions?

If you have interviewed some dream characters and personifications of your life issues, ask them about your doubts.

7: Discovering an Authentic Plan for Your Life

Students often report that it is easier to create and "become" characters than they expected that it would be. The answers they receive do not feel as if they are coming from "them," but from the character. They also report that the comments made by the character generally make sense, seem appropriate and are helpful. If you are not able to imagine a character, get into role, or get answers, you probably just need practice. It takes a while to develop a genuine, ongoing connection with autonomous perspectives if you aren't used to accessing them.

IDL helps you to align your waking priorities with those that encompass both the realities of your life and your unsuspected potentials so that you can place the needs and wants of your bodies, desires, family, friends, and associates into a context that brings the greatest good for the greatest number. But all too often you will find that you habitually put the priorities of your waking identity first. Here is a metaphor to explain the problems that can cause. Imagine that you are an iceberg floating happily near the Arctic circle, back before global warming made them a historic oddity. It's snowing and you are surrounded by your companion icebergs. The water all around you is covered with ice and there is a hard wind blowing against you from the south, ensuring that you will float north where it is cold. What a great life!

As you look ahead into the future, you have every reason to expect that it is going to be wonderful. But tomorrow, with the first light of day, you notice that you are a little farther from your friends and you have floated a little to the south. This is very strange! After all, the wind is blowing fiercely *from* the south. You should be even farther north! A week goes by. Every day your friends seem a little farther away. Sure, it's still well below freezing, but it's not snowing as much now and, unless you are imagining things, the water doesn't seem quite as cold. The ice that used to cover the surface is long gone. What's going on?

A month goes by. You can't see any of your friends. Although the wind continues to blow fiercely from the south, the water is definitely warmer. You seem to be shrinking! With this realization, disillusionment sets in. Things are not working out the way they should! Despite all the signs that indicate that the weather should be getting colder, it is getting warmer! Despite all the signs that point to you having more friends, you have none at all! You are alone, out in the middle of a huge ocean, without any snow! Life isn't fair! As you shrink day by day, you become more embittered, angry at the world for cheating you out of your happiness and your future.

What happened to this iceberg? Why didn't life live up to its expectations? Was life unfair? What do you think? From the perspective of the part of the iceberg *above the water*, this is certainly a fair and accurate accounting of reality.

However, the perspective of the tip of the iceberg only represents ten percent of the reality of the iceberg as a whole. The tip was speaking for the whole of the iceberg, but did its world view match that of the greater part of its being? The tip of the iceberg was simply out of touch with the ninety percent of itself that was below the surface of the water. As a result, it remained unaware of the slow, gentle, consistent and persistent push of a southerly current on its underwater mass. If it had been aware of *all* of its being, it would have understood its destiny and how it fit into the natural order of things. It would not have experienced its life in a way that was based on unrealistic expectations and therefore concluded that life wasn't fair. It would not have spent its time feeling confused, sad, and angry. Instead, it would have made the most of the life it had.

You find yourself in a similar predicament. Like the iceberg, you focus on that part of your life that you are aware of - your waking life. You make decisions based on the winds of opinion, fortune, and habit that blow in your waking world, rarely if ever considering those subtle and deep life currents that move the greater mass of your being. Consequently, should you be surprised when your life does not work out according to your expectations? Isn't this rather the natural outcome of living a life cut off from the agenda of the larger part of who you are? Your life compass takes into account your waking self, your retrospective roles and creates opportunities for unrecognized potentials to emerge.

After all, why should you recognize them if they are not part of your self-definition and are new to your experience?

Why should you expect or understand them when they are more than who you are and your current world view? Trying to run your life from just your limited waking perspective is like trying to drive a car with only a steering wheel but no brakes or accelerator. Fortunately, getting in touch with the priorities of your emerging priorities is both natural and easy. For example, Julie came to an overnight dream incubation workshop that I offered. She had recently turned thirty and was unmarried. She felt her biological clock ticking and was frustrated that she had been unable to find the right partner. She wanted to incubate a dream about this issue. The next morning Julie woke me up early and excitedly told me the following dream. "I am in my wedding gown walking down the isle of an enormous church with my husband to be! He is wearing a black tux. I can't see his face. I look up at the walls of the church and there are spider webs everywhere! Then I look down at my gown and there are spiders crawling all over it, weaving webs! I am horrified and wake up, shocked!"

What would you make of this dream if you had it? Julie thought that it might be warning her that marriage was a bad thing for her and that perhaps she should give up on ever finding an appropriate partner. When we talked to the church it said, "I am the spiritual part of Julie's life. These spiders have their home in me. I like them." The spiders said, "We are beautifying our home and Julie's dress with our beautiful webs. Julie is focusing way too much on finding a mate. She is a spiritual artist and she has been neglecting her artwork, which expresses her spirituality. If she will focus on expressing the priorities of her authentic self through her spiritual art, this business of finding a mate will take care of itself."

Julie was amazed at this. She stated that she had indeed been an artist and loved to create spiritually-themed works, but that she had stopped doing so some time ago because it seemed so unrelated to finding the right guy and settling down. What the church and spiders said felt right to Julie and she decided that she would take their advice. She decided that she was going to return to making her artwork a priority,

About eighteen months later Julie came up to me with a male friend. She introduced me to Tom, her fiancé! She told me that after the dream incubation she had returned to her artwork and had attempted to put marriage out of her mind. It was in the course of building her life around her spiritual artwork that she met Tom.

This story illustrates how IDL encourages not so much insight into yourself, like much psychotherapy does, or practical problem-solving, like most coaching does, or instruction in a pre-set discipline, as most religions and spiritual paths do, but instead emphasizes deep listening to the priorities of emerging potentials. As you choose to live out of perspectives that transcend and include your own you attract to yourself those people and life experiences that are in harmony with them.

Sometimes issues that don't look like they are at all related on the surface share the same root system deep down within us. Somehow Julie's focus on spiritually-motivated artistry was a priority that needed to be addressed in order for her love life to work out.

We can also see from this example how limited our waking understanding of dreams can be. Most people immediately find a church with cobwebs and a wedding gown covered with spiders and their webs creepy, if not downright scary. In IDL, there is a place for interpretation and projection of our assumptions onto dreams, and that is both before we interview dream characters, when you say why you think you had the dream, as well as afterward when you interpret the entire interview and decide what you want to do with it.

However, you can see how misinterpretation normally starts during a dream or lucid dream itself: we see spiders in a church and draw wrong conclusions; instead of suspending our assumptions, asking questions and practicing deep listening, we practice deep projection, drawing incorrect assumptions and then reacting in ways that can turn the dream, lucid dream or our waking life into a nightmare.

IDL teaches you to focus on a much more basic, much more important goal than insight into a dream or lucid dream, and that is transformative, direct, and personal interaction with it. You really can't say with any degree of confidence what a feeling, dream, or physical symptom is about unless you first consult those perspectives that are at least as invested in those issues as *you* are. Isn't that true about the church, spiders, and their webs? Are they not at least as invested in the dream as the dreamer is? You learn, with much practice with IDL, to hold your opinions, interpretations, and projections in abeyance in favor of listening to the input and perspectives of various interviewed characters. As they practice IDL, what comes up again and again for people is a shift in emphasis, similar to what we see in the story of the iceberg.

There is a shifting of agendas from waking goals that we *assume* speak for our greatest good – in this case, protection from the threat of spiders - to priorities that *actually* reflect our greater good – the perspectives embodied by the spiders, webs, and church.

While awareness of life itself evolves throughout development, the levels of authenticity that lie beyond your sense of self fall into three categories. These are energy, beingness, and formlessness, often referred to as the psychic, subtle, and causal, or the path of yogis, the path of saints, and the path of sages.

IDL associates abundance with the first, cosmic humor with the second, and luminosity with the third.

On the level of energy, you experience oneness with all life as flows of energy and as oneness with nature. "Energy medicine, " chakras, the holographic universe, psychism, most archetypes, and quantum anything reflect energy-centered perspectives of oneness. One dreamer, Martha, was afraid of the destructive power of a huge tornado storming over her city. When she became the tornado she discovered that it personified a perspective that owned her energy and her power, which was something that she herself did not do. By practicing being the tornado at important moments of her day Martha stopped being self-critical about the chaos that sometimes accompanied her daily life. She realized that when she authentically lived who she was and assumed the perspective of the tornado, she re-owned her energy and power and accessed it in ways that were new to her. As a result, Martha was much more effective in her ability to serve others and to meet her own needs.

When Margaret was a girl she dreamed about a fairy. It said, "I am a joyful, angelic energy. I am really happy, lively, other-worldly energy. I'm singing. Margaret said, "What are you?" The energy said, "I am the soul of a beautiful singer. I am here to remind Margaret of her divine heritage. Be aware! Look at the situation from a nice high perspective. Just be very grateful. Just be SO thankful!" This is another example of experiencing life from a perspective of sacred, natural energy. Love of life, the vitality of exercise and sports, sex, nature, and the environment, are important manifestations of this realm.

IDL emphasizes the abundance associated with this level because it constitutes an awakening to the unbounded possibilities of life, when we become one with it.

This is demonstrated in IDL by the unlimited abundance not only of perspectives with which to identify, but with the abundance of support that is continuously and immediately available, regardless of what our concerns may be.

From perspectives of the second transpersonal level, others are not only harmonious expressions of energy but of empathy that inspires a life of service.

Life is experienced as The Beloved with whom we must become one through

41

service, devotion, prayer, and meditation. As a point of focus, oneness with energy is transcended and included in an experience of oneness with the sacredness of all being, however we may conceive it, through love, devotional rapture, bliss, and a life directed by divine grace. A Christian will experience it as oneness with Christ while a Sufi will experience oneness with Allah. Whatever your waking assumptions are about the nature of the sacred, of Beingness and reality, you will experience yourself becoming one with them. Life as experienced from this level is about devotion to the beloved, and the beloved is seen as everyone and everything. This level of authenticity transcends spiritual forms such as angels, divine masters, and God as a personality because the seeker has become one with *all* archetypes. As focus moves from forms toward oneness with those core intentions that give meaning to all experience, brilliant, ecstatic lights and sounds may replace energy as experiences of oneness in meditation. Many of the experiences reported by near death experiencers are of oneness with energy and love.

Romance is a lower level echo of this realm, in that we seek unity through devotion to another person and experience consummation of that devotion in our experience of oneness with them. However, rather than imagining that the authenticity of transpersonal devotional union through service is a state of constant bliss, it is more realistic to think of it as a life lived in oneness with your most central and inclusive intentions. When two people live together who are one in mind, body, and emotions, life is not experienced as constant bliss or constant romance, nor should it be. Instead, life is experienced as a mutual, interdependent support of the other in a shared life adventure.

Mary dreamed of a glorious golden light shining out from a tower. It said, "I am a beacon of light and hope. My light shimmers. There is gold!

My strengths are that I provide safety, protectiveness, and mental health. I am Mary's guide for her future. If I were in charge of Mary's waking life, I would have her check with me.

When she sees me in her mind's eye, she is on the right path. If she does not see me, that is a sign not to go that way. She is most likely to see me and use me to help her make almost any type of decision.

If she gets hung up on a decision, she needs to become me, the beacon of light." Mary found that by becoming the light whenever she was not sure which way she needed to go, she became clearer, more confident, and more directed.

Notice that a lighthouse is a rather obvious personification of the concept of one's inner or life compass; when Mary listens to it and makes its priorities her own she is radically expanding her world view. Mary is not giving up her waking priorities; they are not in conflict with those of the lighthouse. Instead, its priorities both include and transcend her own, accepting her priorities while creating contexts that only broader priorities can.

Steve had a repetitive dream that brought him to much the same realization. In it he was driving in circles in a big city, not sure where he was going and encountering one traffic jam or confusing detour after another. How would it feel to spend a night dreaming such dreams?

How would it likely affect how you felt in the morning, whether or not you remembered your dreams? How would it make you feel about dreaming? The problem was that Steve and his world view were driving the car, and his life priorities were taking him around in stressful circles. The solution came when Steve suspended his need to interpret and control the dream and instead practice deep listening to the perspective of the car that he was driving.

When he did so the answer became very clear. The car didn't want to change, nor did it find anything wrong with the city. In fact, it did not care where it was driven. However, it suggested that what Steve needed to do was simply buy and use GPS! This solution caused Steve to focus on what his preferred destination was. Where was he trying to get to in his life? He had been thinking about finding a house in the country and moving there, where he could have a life with more tranquility and less stress. The Car (and now the Navi, which he interviewed) both supported this decision and suggested that before he went to sleep at night that he input his desired country destination into his dream car Navi!

The result was not only the elimination of these stressful, futile, and draining repetitive dreams, but restful, regenerative sleep, awakening with a sense of lightness, enthusiasm, and optimism, because now Steve felt like he was "on track" with his life, "on his path," although he was not sure what that was or where exactly he was headed. Somehow, it didn't seem to matter so much any more.

IDL associates cosmic humor with the subtle or "beingness" level for several reasons. Experiences of this level are so beatific, loving, compassionate in their all-embracing oneness that people come away convinced that they have experienced and now know Truth, Reality, and God. The cosmic humor in this is that these revelations, while profound, are dependent on the perceptual contexts of the perceiver, something few of them recognize. They therefore take partial and limited enlightenment to be absolute and ultimate enlightenment, because they cannot conceive that it could ever possibly be outgrown. Cosmic humor occurs when we take ourselves and our fervent convictions too seriously, when we personalize life when it has nothing to do with a self that is also a figment of our imagination.

Cosmic humor is obvious in almost every IDL interview. That not only common sense but useful suggestions can come from imaginary chipmunks, garbage can lids, and pterodactyls is cosmically humorous, in that it demonstrates how the irrational, when combined with reason, can easily produce trans-rational openings. The more the self is thinned the more humorous the delusion of the self becomes, and IDL supports and enhances this thinning of the self in several effective ways.

The most refined level of self-centered awareness is so ineffable that it cannot even be called "subtle" anymore. Because it is without any form at all, even light, blackness, or space, it is called the "causal" level, out of which all form, all ideas, all feelings, all things, all dream images emanate. Think of it as the realm of the laws that directed the creation of the universe. Such patterning principles must preexist the forms that express their nature. Oneness on this level transcends and includes not only oneness with energy, but both the experience of oneness with God and the experience of Self.

It is not that there is no God or no Self, but that from the perspective of the formless these are experienced as descriptive and experiential tools rather than as absolute realities.

For example, as a tool, your hand has no meaning or use apart from your body. Similarly, from a causal perspective the experience of self is seen as a tool for the manifestation of life rather than as an absolute reality. God and Self are, from this perspective, just two more roles. This approaches what Buddhism is conveying when it speaks of *annata*, "no self," and why it refuses to discuss the reality of God.

As a causal level religion, it does not view these perspectives as ultimately real or conducive to final enlightenment, although they remain both relevant and useful to life in the real world.

You may have had a dream, mystical or near death experience in which God appeared or was experienced in one way or another.

Because the producer and director of a play is a broader perspective than that of any particular character in the dream, including God, becoming the perspective of the producer of the dream provides an even broader perspective than that of any and all dream characters, including God. Such a perspective does not feel like a character in the dream; it is a clear witness that transcends all preferences, neither loving nor hating, yet not at all indifferent.

In IDL, such a perspective is called "Dream Consciousness," and refers to the world view that contains and therefore transcends all the preferences expressed by all the characters in the dream. It is causal because it personifies the creativity and life that generates dreams, identity and life.

In relationship to you it is a lucid perspective, and when you become it, whether awake, asleep, dreaming, lucid dreaming, or in an altered state of consciousness, you become lucid, awake, and relatively enlightened. IDL has tools for accessing this perspective.
[11]

IDL associates the formless, causal realm with luminosity in order to emphasize

---

11 For example, Dream Sociometry is a form of IDL that interviews a cross-section of characters from a dream or life issue, accessing their preferences as numerical values that can be plotted on a Dream Sociogram to depict the interactional patterns of these various perspectives and their preferences. In addition, various commentaries explain these preferences and elaborate on their significance and relevance for the life of the dreamer. One perspective that can be interviewed by this process is "Dream Consciousness," or the perspective that created the dream in ist entirety. For more information, see http://integraldeeplistening.com/dream-sociometry/.

the clarity, lucidity, and wakefulness, but without content or a sense of self. This luminosity is the font of creativity, the realm from which emerging potentials spring. It is "Dream Consciousness," the entirety of holonic quadrant factors that generate dream content.

By implication, it is also "Life Consciousness," the entirety of holonic quadrant factors that generate life.

Experiencing formless awareness is a powerful aid to meditation and for the expansion of clarity in general because it provides a direct and personal experience of your life compass that is otherwise almost impossible to communicate. It can be attained through years of meditation or it can be Typically, it is stumbled upon through drug, mystical, shamanic or near-death experiences. These are notoriously difficult to duplicate, leaving some people pining for "home" but having no idea how to get there. The result is that they can detach from the less real, less meaningful existence of their everyday life and become chronically depressed.

Of course meditation is designed to access clear, formless, lucid enlightenment, but many people lack the

motivation, method, and discipline to succeed. When they do, they may go years before they have the experience again.

IDL provides a simpler, more direct, and more easily duplicable way to access all three levels of transpersonal awareness, and beyond them, what is called the "non-dual." While encouraging meditation and supporting other paths as part of one's ongoing integral life practice, IDL suggests that supplementing those approaches with IDL interviewing will both enhance their efficacy and increase the likelihood that direct transpersonal experiences are likely to be encountered through interviewing emerging potentials.

You can use IDL to return to these experiences again and again until they are stabilized in your ongoing daily experience as your everyday mind. For example, Martina shared the following life issue: "I feel very paralyzed by world events: disappearing animals, arms race, child prostitution. It makes me feel that we don't have a lot of time and that keeps me from living a full life. I have dread about the near collapse of the planet."

She then shared the following: "I dreamed I was overhead looking at the coast of a continent. It looked like Asia. Over it was a dark shadow.

Then I was on the ground looking up at it. I determined that there were four layers of this shadow, which was like looking through cellophane. Then I saw the bust of a woman. She had on a black sweetheart strapless dress. She reached in between her breasts and pulled out what looked like a bazooka! I didn't know how she could possibly have something like that in that little dress! She shot straight up through the shadow cloud so that light would come through."

Martina's associations to the dream were as follows: "What's going on in Korea is really dark, more dark than probably what I've read. The implications of the cloud being over Korea, Russia, and China is very scary. Maybe Japan too. That

45

might be the four levels. It is an interesting idea that out of the heart chakra or out of the breasts of a woman would come a weapon to shoot through it. I was amazed at the aggression that came up because I am not a violent woman; but I can understand the violence I could feel toward a nuclear threat to our planet.

I was using some sort of energy from my heart. I looked up "gun" later and it had to do with some sexual energy, so I can imagine that it would be some sort of serious energy that I would be shooting toward this encroaching darkness."

What would you make of this dream if you had it? It is the kind of apocalyptic revelation that create belief in Armageddon or literal prophesies foretelling the End of the World. As such, these experiences are powerful enough to unite masses of humans in obedience to misunderstandings, misinterpretations, projections and lives built around delusional myths. By acting out their projected fears they bring to pass that which terrorize them.

What perspectives might the dream itself provide? When we interviewed the cloud it said, "I'm sheer dark. I'm easily seen through. I'm good, beautiful, and mysterious. I'm definitely over a coast and not over any particular country. It's comfortable to me to be over the edges of things that are different – land and water—because those edges are very rich in diversity. Regarding the woman who shoots me, it just helps me to see another part of myself; with the empty light going between different parts of myself I get to see the Earth better, see above me better, see a little circle of emptiness. It's very exciting. I like it!"

"I don't fear destruction and so everything above and below me is a blessing. It's beautiful! I am not worried about myself. I am quite satisfied and pleased with what I am. A limitation that I have is that I can't always communicate myself to others or even be seen by others. I most closely personify things Martina sees but doesn't know or understand yet."

Notice that because the dark clouds are emerging potentials for Martina they are misunderstood; she has no way to categorize or classify them apart from listening to them and allowing them to teach her how to do so. If she does not, her innate human propensity for control will tend to perceive it as a threat and react to it in a defensive way.

The clouds continued: "If I could change this dream I would have a unifying conversation or relationship between the woman and me so that they would become more one and enjoy each other.

Then I would feel less separation, more union with myself and surroundings."

"If I were in charge of Martina's waking life I would have her wear black more, more like a satin black as kind of a power statement, but in a feminine way. I would have her tune into me all the time. She could refer to the black in her outfit and think of the way I look and she will be tuned in. If she tunes in to me, things will be more shear, more clear, less her own decisions or her own responsibility."

Martina is here being given predictions that she can test. The cloud is predicting that if she wears black more often she will become clearer, more lucid, and will personalize life less.

"Regarding Martina's sense of dread, I feel like I'm bigger than that. I don't feel like I need the planet to survive. As far as she's concerned, since she's on the planet...I can offer her and her family safety if that would help. I can give her direction to maintain that safety. In that way she can move on. I would provide safety through the hole made by the bazooka, which is like a little spotlight that gives her a direct connection with something that will guide her. The messages that are received will keep her path very safe. If she chooses to protect the planet in some way, then those guidelines will come."

Here the cloud is claiming that it is a personification of Martina's life compass that can give her direction to help her maintain her sense of safety.

The cloud is thereby showing empathy with Martina.

Although it does not feel unsafe, it recognizes that in order to grow, Martina needs to feel safe, and it offers her tools to do so.

On a scale of zero to ten, the cloud scored itself as a "ten" in confidence, empathy, wisdom, acceptance, equanimity, and witnessing.

It added, "I recommend that Martina imagine that she is me when she sleeps, when she works, and when she interacts with God. It would probably take some meditation and journaling. It will take a couple of months for her to integrate me.

Cloud, do you think that the Earth is collapsing or do you think it is just a fear in Martina?

"I think it is both. Unless all reports and visuals are false, it's very clear that there's destruction going on to the ecosystem of our planet. Also, it is a fear of Martina's. She could focus on a lot of other things. So I would say both."

What does the color black mean to you?

To me as a cloud? It's like the night and it's like outer space. It's able to shine like a black pearl. Not too many people think of it that way. It's a place where you can have quiet and solitude. There's something sacred about black. It's what was before there was light. It's incalculable. There's no time to it. There's no way to judge it. It's just a point where things either explode into being or condense into non-being. It's just part of the elegant everything. It's not something that I can have a feeling about."

Here we have a direct experience of identification with the formless transpersonal and its attempt to describe itself.

You appeared as scary, not directing and comforting. Why?

"Using Martina's fear was a strong way of getting to her so she would remember, waking her up. I didn't mean for it to cause any damage; I just knew that it would be a really good way to get her up and remember." This is a common theme in nightmarish IDL interviews. The intention is often stated as a need to wake up the dreamer, and if scaring them is required to do so, life doesn't care.

While this stance could be viewed as callous and immoral, it is more accurately described as transcendent, detached, and amoral.

Martina was moved emotionally by her interview and her encounter with the perspective of the cloud. She felt that she experienced a part of her that was

47

normally so foreign to her that it was routinely misperceived as a threat.

This experience helped Martina to remove blocks to growing into oneness with the causal dimension of her consciousness.

Exercises

What are your waking priorities?

Are the priorities of dream characters and personifications of your life issues that score high in the six core qualities of your authentic self (see next chapter) in agreement?

If they are not, do you know what to do

8: Six Core Qualities of Your Authentic Self

There are at least six core authentic qualities that express themselves again and again in the context of the emerging potentials that you interview. These are confidence, empathy, wisdom, acceptance, inner peace or equanimity, and witnessing. There are other core authentic qualities, such as compassion, humor, thankfulness, joy, and power, but I recommend that you focus on these six as keys to the others. This is because they are grounded in the essence of what it means to be alive: the six parts of the cycle of every breath you take: your abdominal and chest inhalations, the slight pause at the "top" of each breath, your chest and abdominal exhalations, and the longer pause at the "bottom" of each breath. These qualities are therefore embedded in the fundamental fabric of life, first as direct, personal experiences, then as processes, then as qualities, and finally as thoughts, feelings, and actions that embody them. They exist as latent or expressed potentials in all roles, whether retrospective, personal, or prospective, but they become stronger and clearer as your identity expands and includes more and more of life. Eventually they become more real than things, ideas, and people. Dream characters and personifications of your life issues are often asked to rate themselves zero to ten for each of these six qualities, just as Cloud did in Martina's interview, to provide their own evaluation of how they rate in each of these areas. Prospective characters typically score themselves higher than we ourselves do on at least some of them.

Confidence

Confidence is an innate characteristic of the audacity of the emergence of life. It is an outgrowth of the rebirth that every abdominal inhalation brings to the body. Think of the germinating of a seed, opening in darkness and moving up through the soil into the light of day. On a physical level we are used to thinking about this as impulse, or blind instinctual urges, or the mechanistic playing out of biological encoding.

However, it is difficult to ignore the audacity of entropy in a world that is supposed to be ruled by the second law of thermodynamics, which decrees that everything naturally moves by inertia into a state of maximum random dispersal. The behavior of a germinating seed is anything but this. As such, it represents birth and rebirth, awakening, resurrection, and even enlightenment. The quality or value that is fundamental to all such negentropic eruptions – of which our nighttime dreams are one example – is confidence.

The emerging potentials interviewed by IDL do not have material bodies, so they cannot die. Because they have no fear of death, they are confident. To the extent that you identify with such fearless emerging potentials, you experience yourself as deathless.

This does not mean that you should or will not take prudent precautions to protect yourself; it means that when you imagine you are this or that emerging potential that scores high in confidence you will be much less likely to make decisions based on fear of loss, failure, humiliation, rejection, or embarrassment.

How does this principle work? Sara dreamed that beside the road were two giant sweet potatoes. They had fangs, huge teeth, and little legs! They started following her and she was very scared. Imagine – stalked by menacing sweet potatoes! If you had such a dream, what do you think it would mean? Sara couldn't resist interviewing her not-so-sweet sweet potatoes. Both of them said that they were best interviewed as one character. "I am big and fat and look gooey because I don't have any form. I'm ugly. I have little eyes and little legs and a long, fat body.

I am lounging. This is my turf! If anyone comes near I am going to get in their space! If Sara looks at me she can tell I won't be messed with! She intruded into my space, even though she couldn't help it. If I catch her I will attack and bite her. I do it because she's scared! It feels pretty powerful making someone so scared. Normally I feel crabby and bloated. My strengths are that I am intimidating and I won't let anyone mess with me. I'm very solidly present."

The potatoes continued, "I most closely personify Sara's inner self that won't let herself be hurt by anyone. We're her watchdog sweet potatoes! We are so solid: complex carbohydrates! Her heart needs protecting. She thinks she has to be vigilant.

She's scared of me because I'm angry at her for not getting out of the way and letting me do my job, which is to protect her and make sure that she doesn't get hurt."

As she contemplated these words, Sara stated, "Space is a big thing for me. When I feel that other people come into my space I cater to them and don't give myself what I need. But at the same time I'm so protected and guarded that I don't allow myself to be protected by the part of myself that should be allowed to protect me. I also am too much on my guard about things that aren't a threat." The sweet potato pointed this over-reaction to possible threats in a cosmically humorous way. In addition, it said that on a scale of 0-10, with zero being scared all the time and ten being totally fearless, it was a ten in all six qualities!

Sara's sweet potatoes personified a confident, proactive emerging potential that expresses a higher degree of authenticity than she does in her life. By giving it voice Sara made that potential more real, more available and more of a possibility for her in her waking life.

Every now and then death itself shows up as a character in a dream. Death told one dreamer, "I serve as a reminder that a transition from one part of yourself to another is always possible. Of course I'm confident! I can consume fear, anger, or most anything else. On the other side of me comes healing." Confidence comes as we outgrow irrational fears of death and come to understand that the passing of relationships and the body are necessary for rebirth.

In Margaret's dream, Fire said it most closely personified "a part of Margaret that burns dross and clears old energy and old things away so you can move on. That power to clear out is always poised, ready to come into Margaret's life with an invitation. That sort of powerful cleansing needs to be invoked every once in while." Once you understand that life itself, as personified by such high scoring emerging potentials, cannot die, it is possible to embrace transformations that would otherwise terrify us.

A good friend of mine suddenly lost a business partner and ally in his spiritual growth. He was overcome with grief. When the grief was given a color and then a shape it became the all-devouring bodhisattva Mahakala of Tibetan Buddhism. Mahakala was eating everything – his grief, his fear for the future, even his anger at death. In the emptiness that followed, my friend was finally able to find inner peace and a way forward with his life.

Stephanie dreamed that she jumped into a canal full of snakes to rescue a skier. When we interviewed the snakes they said, "We personify Stephanie's fears. We grow stronger when we are taken to the light and understood rather than feared. We bring an inner wisdom, insight, and understanding of self. As she listens to her inner voice we will partner with her and help her to heal. She won't be surprised by issues popping up any more. She'll feel more complete and more accepting."

Because Rosanne had fear show up as a common element in many dreams we chose to interview it. We asked her, *Rosanne, if fear was a color, what would it be?*

"Orange. The fear is a vivid orange."

If fear became an object or thing, animate or inanimate, what would it be?

"I am a hot, orange fire… I am flame. Fear is FLAME."

Flame stated, "I am powerful but harmless flame. I have a cool and hot side with blue in me. I am free. Rosanne is afraid; she has fear. She's afraid of being alone. What I like most about myself is that I have freedom. It's hard to describe but I can do what I want. I can be any shape I want. I can go anywhere. I don't need windows. I leap when I want to go somewhere. I like my heat. My heat represents love. It's just love and I like myself. I wouldn't change anything about me. I have unlimited strengths.

Rosanne is resisting my strength. She's not accepting it. In Rosanne 's dreams I would not have her running. I would have her trust and not be fearful. If she just walked and trusted she would find her path. If I could live Rosanne's waking life for her, I would be more assertive and speak up. Rosanne fears people will not love her if she speaks her truth. She would discover it wouldn't matter… nothing bad would happen. Because Rosanne has so much anxiety, it would help her to release that and come forward if she imagined she was me. People would feel the warmth and love that she gives. Rosanne would not feel the rejection she fears."

While Rosanne rated herself three on a scale of zero to ten for fearless confidence, flame rated itself as ten.

All of these examples demonstrate the confidence that naturally occurs when fear is listened to, accepted, and responded to in a respectful way. Such confidence is a necessary pre-requisite for the transformation you want to occur in your life. It will strengthen naturally when you practice IDL regularly.

Empathy

In earlier versions of IDL, compassion was the second of the six core qualities. The thinking that chest inhalation provides additional oxygen, and therefore life, than that which is provided automatically by abdominal inhalation. As such, it personifies not only aliveness, but an ability to give back through a love that ripens into compassion.

However, many interviewed emerging potentials that consistently scored high in the other five core qualities scored themselves low or zero on compassion. Why?

Essentially, compassion is a human expression of caring and while emerging potentials may be human creations and have human attributes, they themselves are not human, in that they are not alive, have bodies, and physical security needs and cannot die, nor do most say they want to human!

They have nothing against compassion; it simply doesn't accurately describe the way most perceive life. Is that simply a reflection of the non-evolved consciousness of most people who have done IDL interviews?

If so, then those emerging potentials that do score themselves high in compassion would be more evolved than those that do not. However, neither the interviews nor the individuals interviewed seem to support this conclusion. This created a challenge. If compassion was not the core quality that was associated with chest inhalation and aliveness, what was? In time the answer became obvious. Because interviewed emerging potentials are in part aspects of the person who is interviewed, they know them better than another person or a purely external force possibly could. This complete knowledge is an innate, higher-order empathy. But because emerging potentials transcend humans, in that they are creative perspectives that are relatively autonomous and detached from humanity, they are often less invested in morality than humans, because morality is in part a social construct which humans need to structure interaction.

This sounds cold, immoral and even threatening to many humans, who cannot conceive of any life worth living, any enlightenment worth possessing, that is not centered on love and compassion.

Therefore, IDL is not for everyone. Those who feel compelled to choose between their own preferences and those of emerging potentials will probably retain their own.

However, this is a false choice. Neither IDL nor emerging potentials force such a choice on its students. Be human! Be loving! Be compassionate! Use IDL to support and balance your growth in these areas.

52

As has been noted above, empathy is an essential line of human development because the ability to take the role of others is a prerequisite to the development of love, compassion, and higher-order morality. People who lack empathy simply do not have the option to grow in these ways. The fact that emerging potentials naturally have such a high degree of empathy implies that they also have attained a high degree of love, compassion, and morality. Have they? Look at your own interviews and draw your own conclusions.

Juanita, who came to our Integral Salon one Sunday night said, "In my dream there was an earthquake and our house cut loose and went out to sea. I was alone in the house. I don't swim. I don't know how I made it to shore." What would you think such a dream would mean if you had it? When we interviewed the ocean it said, "I am salty and create buoyancy. I am able to keep Juanita up. I am very proud of myself for being able to do that. I generate swells underneath her so she can stay up."

Juanita realized from this experience that regardless of the trials and tribulations of her life that there was at least one perspective, and probably others that she had not yet discovered, that always cared about her and supported her.

Because she had not recognized it or had confidence in it, the ocean functioned as an emerging potential for Juanita – as a healing and transformative place from which she can live her life, but which she has to grow into. While we might call the ocean compassionate, it did not see itself that way. It was just being itself and doing its job as an ocean! It did not see itself as compassionate. However, its comments demonstrated that it had a clear empathy with Juanita's need to be supported.

Louise, who dreamed about Spit, was surprised when it said, "I am tired of being spit. I am a gooey, nasty thing. I would want to form Louise into an inner beauty that would be untouchable from the harm she causes herself. She would no longer think that she is small and worthless. She would enjoy her life."

Louise was amazed to discover that Spit had more compassion and caring toward her than she did toward herself.

However, the Spit itself did not see itself as compassionate. Instead, it was just being Spit. However, intrinsic to Spit's nature, as partially an aspect of Louise, was complete empathy with her perspective, dramas, dilemmas, desires, and hopes.

Empathy tends to broaden and deepen naturally as one practices IDL. This may be due to a consistent suspension of judgments about dream characters and personifications of your life issues; it may be due to the growth in empathy that accompanies regular practice in taking the role of the other.

It may be due to putting into practice in your daily life the recommendations of emerging potentials that are themselves highly empathetic. Because IDL deepens the realization that we are all interdependent and that all others both aspects of ourselves and yet autonomous, you will naturally grow in your desire to treat others as you want to be treated. You will naturally want to look beyond the limitations of humanity, of personas and beliefs, to the underlying beauty of those emerging potentials that shine forth from within all people.

Wisdom

Wisdom is clear, detached awareness, an intuitive knowing that leads to being in the right place at the right time, to do or say that which will awaken a higher, broader, deeper reality within other people. It is an outgrowth of the life balance that is represented by the pause between every inhalation and every exhalation, a balance of alertness and relaxation, of male and female, of autonomous action and collective nurturance, of day and night. It takes wisdom to grow and maintain balance, and the ability to stay balanced generates higher orders of wisdom.

An ocean told one dreamer, "I have been around for millennia, so I can give you ancient wisdom." Wisdom is different from mere knowledge, which separates life into the knower and known. Wisdom is simple awareness, yet it is endowed not only with the degree of consciousness of the person being interviewed, but with the wisdom innate to its own perspective.

Therefore, its consciousness is not the same as the simple awareness of a rock or a plant or a baby. Wisdom is not colored by emotional preferences, yet it is not dismissive or unaware of them either.

It takes feelings into account and balances them with reason, the needs of others, personal ability, and the limitations and possibilities inherent in the environmental context.

A mirror in Linda's dream said, "I personify her wisdom. My strengths are being reflective, having an inner knowing, a quiet strength.

I am in this dream to help her connect with me. She doesn't know how to very well. She can do so by being quiet and reflective." By imagining herself once again becoming the mirror at those times when she felt reactive and stressed out, Linda found herself more "reflective," with an inner knowing of how to respond to the situation.

Andrea dreamed she was having a baby. Her baby said, "I personify Andrea's deepest, true self. I am her true self that is ready to be nurtured in the world and by herself too. My strengths are 'the wisdom of goal vision' and trusting a heck of a lot more. At this point I can see Andrea as more trusting than at any other time in her life." Andrea practiced imagining she was the baby when she found herself worried that she was off track in her life direction. Andrea had discovered an emerging potential o r muse that helps her access "the wisdom of goal vision."

A Hawk in Ellen's dream said, "I flew into the back seat of Ellen's car to be near her. She knows and understands me. She won't harm me. I am here to let her know that I can see her. What I like about myself is that I can fly really high. When I'm way up in the sky I can see everything at a wide angle and I don't have tunnel vision. I can see the tiniest mouse in the field. I personify Ellen's inner sight that is the same as mine. She can see underneath the surface of things. If she could see like me all the time she would have a knowing.

She would see that there is no harm done by the coyotes chewing on the tips of the antlers in her dream." Ellen was a native American; the hawk told her that the coyotes chewing on the tips of antlers in her dream was a reference to her concern about the deterioration of her people's spiritual traditions. From the Hawk's perspective, this was not something for Ellen to worry about as she pursued her role as a spiritual teacher and healer for her people.

Her dream was a gift of spiritual wisdom about how to be of greater service by accessing her own emerging potentials and helping her people to do the same for themselves.

Ellen also dreamed of an old man sitting outside a house. When she became him she was struck by his wisdom and ability to let go. She had a history of reacting to her mother who still angered her whenever she was around her.

The old man told Ellen to imagine that she was him when she was around her mother. When she followed this advice, she found that she no longer reacted to her mother.

She was becoming an emerging potential, the "old man," which was not attached to an old regressive emotional pattern that was scripted in her youth and that was part of her socialized persona. That pattern of reactivity did not define or relate to who she had the potential to become. This wise prospective emerging potential and spiritual muse helped Ellen to embody wisdom in her dealings with her mother.

A special type of wisdom is seeing a broader picture of what can take place in our lives, something some people call "precognition." There are many incidences of dream characters and personifications of life issues making predictions for the future. For example, the Hawk told Ellen, "I see Ellen doing well off the reservation. She will be doing her work there. It would be better for her that way, in the beginning. Ellen will always be partially off the reservation."

Some predictions by emerging potentials are accurate, some are less so, since their perspectives, while true for each character, do not necessarily correspond to objective truth. This is one reason why we need to check out the wise perspectives of one emerging potential with those of others instead of simply taking what they have to say on faith.

Ellen also dreamed of being in bed with her husband and another man named Al, who she didn't like at all. She was angry at her husband for allowing this situation to exist. The bed was in half of a double-wide mobile home. When Ellen talked to the trailer it said that it was not doing its job of protecting its owners. They were vulnerable and being invaded by Al. Ellen associated this dream to a phone call she received later that same day from a man she had not heard from since she was sixteen or seventeen. He had to see her.

Just before class she met with him and was greatly disturbed when he told her that he was in love with her and had been for years. The mobile home agreed that the dream had been a precognitive depiction of her feelings of vulnerability and the threat this man posed to the intimacy of her relationship with her husband.

Acceptance

Acceptance is easy to associate with the voluntary letting go of breath that occurs when we exhale from the chest. We detach from life; we give it up; we give it away naturally, without a thought. Notice how you feel when you exhale from the chest. There is an automatic movement into a space of deeper acceptance.

If there is any quality that serves as the doorway to living life from the priorities of your emerging potentials, it is acceptance. Acceptance is the ability to acknowledge the good, bad, and the ugly in life and in yourself openly, without reactivity or defensiveness. It has nothing to do with resignation or passivity in the face of injustice.

As you interview emerging potentials with IDL, you will typically find your dream characters and personifications of your life issues to be more accepting of themselves, the actions in the dream, and you, the dreamer, than you are.

Because your dream characters and personifications of your life issues personify aspects of yourself, acceptance of others is basically self-acceptance. Rejection of others is essentially self-rejection. Acceptance implies the presence of such characteristics as patience, cooperativeness, empathy, non-judgmentalness, openness, and receptivity. It does not, however, feel vulnerable, weak, or undiscriminating. A very accepting snake told Neva, a pretty American Indian woman, " If I were in charge of Neva's waking life I wouldn't react. I can leave things alone. I can accept things for the way they are.

If Neva were to do the same through being me, life would be easier for her. Regarding her finances, Neva needs to stop worrying about them, to leave it alone. It's going to get better. Regarding her daughter, Neva needs to pay more attention to herself and how she reacts. She needs to pay more attention and not just sleep on it. I would let her know that the answer she seeks is in front of her."

It is important to understand that acceptance is not to be confused with an "anything goes," relativistic outlook on life. Acceptance is not a passive lack of investment. Think of the sun as being very accepting in that it sends forth its light and warmth regardless of what we think and feel.

However, that does not keep us from getting a sunburn if we are out of alignment with a healthy relationship with the sun. Because we get a sunburn does that mean that the sun is punishing us for breaking the law? No. The sun is accepting; it is not the sun's responsibility that we are out of alignment with a healthy relationship with it.

Margaret dreamed about a fire burning wheat in a field. The fire said, "If I were in charge of Margaret's life I would not have energy to do anything until things reach a certain point. There has to be a period of quiet growth or development until things reach a certain point. I don't need to jump in right now with

56

anything." The fire personified a perspective of patience and the acceptance that things come to fruition in their own time.

Sally was very self critical about being fat. She rated her self-esteem a two on a scale of zero to ten. When she associated a color and then a form with her self-esteem it became a gecko that liked itself a lot. Sally liked to imagine it sitting on her shoulder where it would zap her negative thoughts with its tongue. Because she stopped being so self-critical, she became much more accepting of herself as a person. This helped her to lose weight, because it was no longer an expression of her lack of acceptance of herself.

If you find yourself being critical of others, you are projecting outward your criticalness toward yourself. As you practice IDL you will naturally grow in your acceptance of others. This does not mean, however, that your muses will not call you to a higher standard of loving and living. It does not mean that you will not have expectations of yourself and others. Instead, you will find that your expectations will become more realistic and functional as you become more accepting.

Inner Peace

Abdominal exhalation is a complete surrender into radical freedom. It is the involuntary detachment from all agendas, hopes, fears, and stressors. In the absence of these things radical freedom is accompanied by a state of deep and pervasive peace.

Peace is perhaps the most fundamental, yet the most overlooked, characteristic of life. While peace of mind is something most of us want, few of us make it a priority. This is unfortunate because few things in life can be enjoyed without peace of mind. How can we enjoy health, friendships, prosperity, or happiness without it?

You can have peace without them, but are you happy if you have them but lack inner peace?

Externally focused people tend to view peace of mind as boring. However, there is nothing contradictory about living an active life and having peace of mind at the same time. To do so is to accomplish the alchemy of balance: you are alert and active and relaxed and at peace at the same time. With such balance much is possible; without it, we tend to make the same mistakes over and over again. A river personified how Ellen had a still, slow, quiet personality but could still be very deep and powerful. "She's flowing all right. She is going in the right direction. If you feel that you are dammed up, you can still learn to flow with the current. You can be cleansed and at peace."

An Ocean told Sam, "I would try to make decisions that would make his life easier and suffer less by having him use my calming influence in many life situations. I would use my strength to give him inner strength and power. He has a feeling of helplessness when he realizes he is out of control and is getting buffeted about. I would chart a steady course and flow as easily as I can instead of being in a seething, agitated state."

Many of us have had times in our life when we have felt like we were lost at sea in a small boat, at the mercy of storms that tossed us here and there and threatened to capsize us. Imagine that is happening to you in your life. As a result of this predicament, you spend your life running from bad weather, in search of the comfort and peace of calm waters. Eventually, however, storms come, regardless of where you are. You feel Victimized again, sick of the sea and sick of your life predicament. But what if in your misery you were to notice a small button on the deck of your boat with a sign that said, "Push to submerge?"

It had been there all along, but you hadn't noticed it. Now that you see it, it makes no sense. You think, "If I submerge, I'll drown. That's exactly what I'm trying to avoid!"

And so you spend more years trying to outrun storms and dreading the inevitable next one. In desperation, in the middle of one particularly horrible lightening and thunderstorm at night, while you are rocking up and down in huge swells, in desperation you remember the button. You think, "What do I have to lose by pushing it? I'm going to die in this storm anyway. And if I don't, living like this is miserable."

So in an act of irrational faith, you push the button. To your amazement you watch as clear, curved walls of glass rise up on either side of the boat, coming together above you. Your boat starts to sink! You watch the water come up above the sides as you toss to and fro! You watch as the water covers your little glass canopy and the stormy night sky disappears above you. Perhaps you think, "Oh my God! I'm going to DIE!" As you continue to descend, the rocking and tossing lessens. You do not have to go very deep before it is as peaceful and tranquil as the most pleasant and calm day you have ever experienced on the sea, yet a storm is raging not twenty feet above your head.

Instead of sailing for miles and miles to find calm waters, instead of always fearing the coming of the next storm, you have stumbled on a way to be at peace in the midst of the most violent storms life can bring you. Now you no longer are afraid of storms; now you no longer sail the ocean due to restlessness, a lack of comfort, or out of fear. Instead you are free to be fully present in the here and now, regardless of where you are or what is happening around you.

You will discover that many of your dream characters and personifications of your life issues live and speak out of this serene, meditative place. As you become them, you will learn how to evoke their presence in the midst of the storms of your life. As you do so, you will transform your life.

Witnessing

Take a moment to observe the pause after you exhale and before you inhale. Notice that it is a space of openness and clarity. In that clarity is a detachment that provides a perspective from which to view the entire round of breath. It is part of your breath, but detached from it at the same time.

This is the nature of both clarity and witnessing, or the ability to stand back and watch the drama of your life go by.

Mary dreamed that she was sitting in a plain wooden chair that was over a hole in a field. Her job was to keep the birds from flying up out of the hole. She had just sat down when birds fluttered up out of the hole and fluttered off into the sky. Exasperated, Mary got up and moved her chair over another hole, where the same thing would happen again and again. If you had this dream, what do you think it would mean?

When we interviewed the birds, they said, "We fly where we wish. That chair can't keep us in these holes!"

The birds said that they personified Mary's thoughts and the chair was a metaphor for her new practice of meditation.

They said that Mary was trying to keep her thoughts below the surface of her awareness, suppressing them, when she sat down to meditate. She thought that was what she was supposed to do when she meditated, and it was creating a lot of frustration for her. The birds suggested that she let them fly where they wanted and forget about both them and putting her chair over holes in the field. Why not simply just sit in the field?

By being the birds Mary came to understand that she could simply let her thoughts be and not worry about them, letting them rise and fall in her awareness as they wished. Mary's dream provided an excellent description of cultivating the witness, the ability to watch herself go by. Realizing that we do not have to react to others, to the drama in our lives, to our own feelings and thoughts, is a central contribution of a daily meditative practice. You will find it is also a central characteristic of many of your interviewed emerging potentials. As you identify with them you will find that you naturally come to live your life from the perspective of clear witnessing.

Think of your thoughts, feelings, and physical sensations as types of weather. When you feel good it's like rainbows and blue skies. When you are moody, there are clouds. When you are angry or scared there is thunder and lightening. Now imagine yourself as the sky itself. Somewhere within you all types of weather are happening right now.

There are typhoons, blizzards, thunderstorms, dark, windswept seas, and calm bright days coexisting within you all at the same time. As the sky, do all these different types of weather affect you? Well, they affect how you look, or how you appear, but as the sky you are much greater than any particular type of weather, since you can contain them all simultaneously.

You are aware of all types of weather. You do not judge them. You do not prefer one type over another. All coexist within you as you witness all with equal impartiality. This is a good metaphor with which to approach meditation and the cultivation of witnessing. You are not attempting not to think or feel but rather to cultivate a consciousness that transcends and includes all thinking and feeling.

IDL instruction in meditation encourages you to form your practice around both the recommendations of interviewed emerging potentials and their suggestions about how to go about meditating. The result is that you have an individualized, tailor-made approach to meditation that works for you because it is a response to your particular needs and evolves as you evolve.

Exercises

Rate yourself 0-10 on the following characteristics:

Confidence:
Empathy:
Wisdom:
Acceptance:
Equanimity:
Witnessing:

Now imagine you are the sky. Ask it how it would rate itself on the same six characteristics.

Confidence:
Empathy:
Wisdom:
Acceptance:
Equanimity:
Witnessing:

If you scored higher than the sky on some characteristics, the implication is that it looks to you for support in the cultivation of those qualities. If you scored lower than the sky on other characteristics, the implication is that it is more highly developed than you are and that you would do well to imagine that you are it in those circumstances in which it easily expresses those characteristics in your life.

How would your life be different if, on a scale of zero to ten, you scored ten on each of these six core characteristics of authenticity, on an ongoing basis?

Here is a simple but effective meditation exercise to experiment with:

1) When you inhale, think and feel whatever you want.
2) When you exhale, let go of any thought, feeling, or sensation by expanding your awareness. Become the "sky."
3) At the bottom of the breath simply be clear awareness.
4) Repeat.

9: Freeing Yourself from the Drama Triangle

The Drama Triangle is a concept taken from Transactional Analysis, a choice-based approach to therapy developed in the 1960's by psychiatrist Eric Berne.[12] "TA," as Transactional Analysis is called, emphasizes giving yourself permission to abandon outgrown life scripts and to let go of old roles that block intimacy in communication with others. Life scripts are unconscious beliefs about who you are and what sort of life you will have based on your early childhood experiences. If these are never made conscious and questioned, they continue to direct and control your life.

Psychological drama is emotional and personal investment in a role. When you think you are your roles, such as parent, spouse, boss, employee, or friend, if something happens in a role that you do not like, you will think it is happening to *you*. This is a profound, fundamental, and pervasive misperception that creates untold misery not only in your waking life but in your dreams as well. The drama triangle is composed of three roles, Persecutor, Victim, and Rescuer. A Persecutor is an abuser. You are in the role of abuser when you put your needs before the needs of others and do not take their needs into consideration.

Abusers treat others in ways that they would not want to be treated. They say, "You need to be punished and I'm going to punish you!" "I'll do so by blaming, scapegoating, attacking, or ignoring you." Victims, on the other hand, refuse to accept responsibility. When bad things happen, they are due to someone or something else.

Victims say, "Why does this always happen to ME?" They feel helpless, powerless, and out of control. Alternately, Victims love to wallow in their own incompetence, wailing, "It's all MY fault! I'm no good! I'll never amount to anything!" Rescuers think they are putting the needs of others before their own. They think are just helping others out of the kindness of their heart, but they are not.

The difference between a Rescuer and a helper is that a Rescuer assumes that their help is needed and jumps in without asking for permission while a helper waits for a request. Rescuers "keep on keeping on" without checking to see if their help is appropriate or actually helping. They just assume that what they are giving is what is needed or desired. Rescuers don't stop when the job is done. They assume that they have permission to assist in other ways when they don't. The refrain of Rescuers is, "I work so hard and nobody ever appreciates me!"

---

12 The concept of the Drama Triangle was developed by Stephen Karpman, a teacher of Transactional Analysis.

"After ALL I've done for YOU!!!" If you have ever felt this way, it's a sure tip-off that you were playing the role of Rescuer. You're on the road to burn-out.

There are at least two factors that make the drama triangle a game. First and foremost, it's dishonest. Games have ulterior motives. Whatever role you play, you are being inauthentic unless you are consciously choosing to play that role, and healthy people do not consciously choose to be an abuser, Rescuer, or Victim. If you are consciously choosing to play one of these roles, you are being manipulative, which is also dishonest, unless the other players have agreed to assume such roles as well, as occurs in theatre, board games, and athletics.

Secondly, in both games and the Drama Triangle you inevitably switch roles. If you play one role, you will eventually play them all. If you play the Rescuer you will inevitably be seen as an abuser and feel Victimized. The moral of the story is: play any of these three roles and you'll eventually play all three. While everyone seems to think that they have figured out how to defy this universal psychological law, it is a comfortable delusion.

For example, while a businessman may think, "I'll rip off my customers, offshore jobs, and exploit the environment and get away with it," they themselves are generally blind to the fact that they are in the role of the Persecutor. They generally see themselves as offering valuable services or even doing "God's work."

At the very least, people who choose to live their lives within the Drama Triangle block their personal development through their dishonesty.

The Drama Triangle helps to explain why many people watch TV, go to movies, surf the internet, fall in love, watch and play sports, get divorced, follow the latest and greatest spiritual fad, fight with their families, go to work, and go bankrupt.

Certainly the Drama Triangle is hardly the only motivator for all of these different pursuits and it is conceivable that all of them can be done outside the Drama Triangle. However, once you understand how the Drama Triangle works, you will see it everywhere you look, including in your own dreams. It is a fundamental way that people sabotage their happiness. If you learn to recognize and eliminate it in the three realms of relationships, thinking, and dreaming you will have removed a major barrier to your growth. This is a skill IDL teaches its students.

The *Wizard of Oz* contains terrific examples of the Drama Triangle. Dorothy is a wonderful little Rescuer. She accidentally rescues the Munchkins from the Wicked Witch of the East by crushing her with a falling house. She rescues the Tin Woodman from rust and the Scarecrow from his pole. She even rescues Oz from the hypocrisy of his charade. But, of course the way that she gains our sympathy is because she makes such a wonderful Victim. First, she gets uprooted from her Kansas home by a nasty persecuting tornado. Then she has a highly vengeful witch out to get her. Monkeys come and capture her. She is victimized by the Great and Powerful Oz who is himself a confirmed Rescuer. Dorothy is a poor, helpless Victim who just wants to go home. Because Dorothy chooses to play the Rescuer and the Victim, she also ends up playing the abuser. She gets to smack the Cowardly Lion on the nose, call Oz names, and murder the Wicked Witch of the West.

And what about that Wicked Witch? Apparently Frank Braun, the creator of *The Wizard of Oz,* did not even give her a proper name so as to suitably demonize her. Was she not attempting to bring justice to the person who killed her sister who she saw as a helpless Victim? Might Dorothy be found guilty of two counts of negligent homicide for her part in the killing of two people?

What makes the Drama Triangle powerful is that who is playing what role is a matter of perspective and timing.

Margo shared the following dream that illustrates the power and pervasiveness of the Drama Triangle in our dreams. "I am in a room with a bunch of people that I don't know. Everyone there has been diagnosed as having cancer, including a man who is there. A woman that I am talking to had been diagnosed as having cancer in her left hand that had not spread. I tell her that this idea is very archaic, but why don't you just cut your hand off? Then you don't have to die."

It was pretty obvious to Margo, as it would be to most observers, that the cancer is an abuser. It kills people. When interviewed the cancer confirmed this with remarks such as, "I like a lot that I am inside all these people. That's what I do. That's how I live. I like being in this woman's hand. It won't be long before I'm other places. I love that I'm uncontrollable. I can do anything I want to do. Nobody can stop me. I like the conversation about cutting off her hand. It's amusing. I'll still spread. People should be desperately terrified of me." We can conclude that the cancer is a part of this dreamer that is abusive, plays the role of abuser and Persecutor within the Drama Triangle.

The room, the people, the lady, and the hand all saw themselves as Victims of the cancer in various ways. For instance, the room said, "I don't like the cancer all these people have. That's the reason all this negative energy is inside me. I dislike myself. I feel like I'm full of a bunch of negative energy." Notice that the room feels overwhelmed by something negative that is greater than itself. It feels powerless to do anything about it. The consequence for the room, as is often the case for us, is that we end up not liking ourselves because we feel weak and out of control. The room personifies Margo in the role of Victim in the Drama Triangle.

The dreamer sees herself as a Rescuer. She says, "I love myself. I hate the diagnosis of cancer because it's a bad thing to have cancer. I hate that everybody has cancer because it's bad because it will kill them. I believe that all these people are going to die if they have cancer.

I like the idea of cutting off this woman's hand because it is a solution to stopping the cancer." Rescuers generally have high opinions of themselves because they see themselves as providing the necessary solution. Rescuers are also sure they understand both the problem and what needs to be done to fix it, just as this dreamer does. Since all of these characters are aspects of the dreamer, she is Persecutor, Victim, and Rescuer to herself all at the same time.

This demonstrates the inevitability of assuming the burden of all three roles when we take on any of them, although we do not realize it at the time. It also demonstrates that *you cannot abuse another person without abusing that part of yourself that they personify.* You cannot rescue another person without disempowering the parts of yourself that they personify. You cannot Victimize another person without creating war within yourself. These truths aren't debatable. They aren't opinions.

They are psychic facts that you can and should prove for yourself.

In the Wizard of Oz Dorothy is dreaming. She is most fundamentally Victimized by her ignorance of her own ability to take herself home at any moment. At any time she can choose to step out of the Drama Triangle of her own personal dream and wake up. It is not easy for any of us to get to the place where we realize that all along we have had what we have been searching for. So how do we speed our escape from our own personal Drama Triangle? The answer lies in understanding the toxicity of these roles and moving to a neutral place in relation to them. This place can be called taking on the role of a "helper."

Helpers stop and check to see if their contributions are indeed helpful, effective, and appreciated. Helpers stop and wait for a request for additional assistance instead of automatically assuming that their contributions are needed.

Exceptions are civically sanctioned Rescuers, such as nurses, police, and firemen.[13] Helpers are relatively detached. They have cultivated the witness relative to their own particular life Drama Triangles.

When they play roles in life they do so in order to serve all sentient beings. We have seen that in Buddhism this approach is called *upaya*, or "cunning benevolence." Avatars and Bodhisattvas, in the proper understanding of these roles, are not Rescuers but divine helpers. Helpers also manifest a balance of characteristics that are an antidote to each of the three roles of the drama triangle. These are wisdom, peace, and empathy.

This trinity of core virtues dates back to that axial genius Socrates, who lived in Athens about four hundred years before Jesus. He knew this triad as truth, beauty, and goodness. Truth is not knowledge, which is information collected and understood. A person can be extremely knowledgeable and have little wisdom. Nor should truth be thought of as that which is not false, because what is true today has an unpleasant way of being only partially true tomorrow.

Truth is wisdom, character attained through experiencing the hard lessons of life, either by oneself, or vicariously, by learning through the mistakes of others.

It is easily attained by accessing and becoming emerging potentials. A wise

---

13 People in these roles are not strictly Rescuers because we tacitly give them permission to break down our door or write us a traffic ticket or take off our clothes as part of our social contract. This having been said, people who are drawn to the helping professions often are most comfortable in the role of Rescuer and take up a profession that socially validates that stance. This makes it that much more difficult for them to "wake up" and choose not to be stuck in the Drama Triangle.

person sees that when they play one role in the Drama Triangle they will inevitably play all of them. Because of this awareness they make life choices that extract them from this unconscious merry-go-round of *samsara*. Samsara is the Sanskrit word for misperception, delusion, illusion, and ignorance. Wisdom is recognizing that as we do to others we do to ourselves, because phenomenologically others are personifications of aspects of ourselves. Wisdom is a natural antidote to abuse because people who clearly grasp this principle cannot and do not act out of an intent to abuse others.

When you ask your interviewed emerging potentials how they rate themselves on wisdom, zero to ten, some will be low, but others will be wiser than you are. As you internalize their qualities you not only act more wisely in your waking life but in your dreams as well. The result is that you are less likely to abuse either yourself or others, because you know that to abuse others is to abuse that part of yourself that they represent. This holds true whether you are dreaming or awake.

Peace is a manifestation of harmony, or the proper proportion of things, which is also a good description of beauty. Where harmony exists, peace of mind, balance, emotional tranquility, non-reactivity, and spiritual clarity exist. Peace is an antidote to victimization in that when you will no longer react to your circumstances you no longer experience yourself as a Victim.

Contrary to common opinion, peace is not the absence of conflict but rather the stability that comes from balancing and thereby transcending conflict. Physiologically, such constant conflict is called homeostasis. Without it we get sick and die. Everything is in conflict. Peace is the experience of the higher order integration of lower order oppositions. When we are one with peace we do not react to the roles we necessarily take on in waking and in dreaming.

In a sense we become pellucid toward our lives. Pellucidity is being awake to our dramas without attempting to manipulate, change, or control them, rather like the sky embraces clouds, thunderstorms, and tornadoes with equal equanimity. We simply accept what occurs and respect events and people for what they are.

When you ask your dream characters and personifications of your life issues how they rate themselves on peace of mind, you will again find that some score lower than you do while some score higher. As you listen to the concerns of those characters that are less at peace than you are, you reassure them and cause them to relax and settle down. They feel nurtured and more secure and are therefore less likely to act out. When you experience the peace of emerging potentials that naturally possess more equanimity than you do, you expand your sense of self to assimilate a bit of their broader, more relaxed, less anxious perspective.

Empathy is more than that which is lovable, because what you love may not be good for you. Goodness is at its core the non-detached caring that comes with being able to empathize with all sides of a situation, both good and bad. In the case of the Drama Triangle, empathy witnesses the drama of your identifications with the roles of Persecutor, Victim, and Rescuer without judgment. Empathy is an antidote to playing the Rescuer because when you truly care about other people you see things from their perspective. The result is that you show them love by asking, seeking feedback, and stopping offering support when appropriate.

When you ask dream characters and personifications of your life issues how they score on empathy, you will find that many of them are locked into liking this and disliking that, loving this and hating that. They are controlled by the roller coaster of their emotions, moving from high to low. Others will be narcissistic and unable to empathize. However, you will find other emerging potentials that score higher on empathy than you do. They have more empathy with your life predicament than do you. These muses can provide a depth of support and nurturance that is rare among people. When you become their perspectives, loneliness no longer exists, because you can feel the profound empathy that life, as personified by these emerging potentials, has for you.

Each of these three antidotes has its own dark side. The shadow of truth is ignorance. Ignorance is thinking that you are a self that can die or suffer rejection, loss, pain, or failure. You can discover that this is not true by examining your sense of self.

When you do, you will not find a monolithic immortal "I" but instead roles personifying endless perspectives. Ignorance is also thinking that it is possible to abuse others without doing damage to yourself.

Individuals and systems that emphasize the search for truth, such as science, Hinduism, Buddhism, and philosophy, tend to be blind to their ignorance.

They don't see how they are self-contradictory or damage themselves through their treatment of others. Some examples are the Hindu caste system, scientific experimentation on living beings, the harsh feudal system of traditional Tibetan culture, and in philosophy, self-contradictory proofs of the existence of God or arguments for Just War. All these undercut the credibility of claims to be wise, to know the truth, or what is real.

The shadow of empathy is narcissism, and the root of narcissism is fear. Love-based systems, like Christianity, tend to indulge in the self-abuse of sin and guilt and in a fear of eternal damnation. These are forms of self-persecution within the Drama Triangle. As paradoxical as it sounds, love-based systems tend to be exclusionary. Ken Wilber points out a good contemporary example in the egalitarian and heterarchical stance of postmodern political correctness widely found on college campuses today. While the intent of this perspective is to respect and honor all life by affirming that all people, all cultures, and all behaviors are equal, it comes across as self-righteous, contradictory, and hypocritical because it rejects those approaches that are hierarchical and not egalitarian, because it sees them as inferior to pluralism. Pluralism lacks empathy with non-pluralistic perspectives. Examples would be refusing to call out Israeli apartheid because to do so would be "anti-Semitic," accepting drug abuse because to confront it would be to discriminate against abusers, or to recognize that it is not "anti-feminist" to acknowledge that matriarchal agrarian societies routinely sacrificed babies and were not more highly evolved than patriarchies.

This is a good example of how, by embracing one extreme, in this case equality, we evoke its dark side (rejection of the reality that there is healthy inequality).

The shadow of peace is chaos. Harmony-based systems, like Chinese religion, pacifistic groups, and meditation tend to repress, avoid, and be challenged by imbalance, confusion and disequilibrium. If you build your life around the quest for peace you will tend to fear being off balance and out of harmony.

Many people waste a lot of their lives attempting to find happiness without first securing peace of mind. This does not work because money and good fortune without peace is empty.

Love without peace is tempestuous and unsatisfying. Wisdom without peace has no inner foundation. Health without peace is a mirage and impossible to enjoy. Therefore inner peace is a prerequisite to true enjoyment of any form of happiness.

In your waking life, you switch roles over time. This keeps you from experiencing the inconsistencies and conflicts among roles because they are separated by time and function. A person can go to work at the National Security Agency spying on people and come home and be a dedicated partner and parent without any apparent cognitive dissonance. This separation of roles can even keep you from realizing that you are playing one or another of the roles of the Drama Triangle. Dreams dissolve the Drama Triangle by collapsing the three roles of Rescuer, Victim, and abuser into one time and one identity. In your dreams you also experience yourself in all three roles, but with this critical difference: you experience yourself in all three roles *at the same time* in the context of other parts of yourself. If you dream of a roaring fire about to consume you, you are the Victim of yourself as the fire, which is your role as Persecutor, and you are your Rescuer when you change to another dream or wake up. Therefore, when you play one role, you play them all; when you experience another dream character as playing the role of persecuting monster, you are merely scaring and persecuting yourself. IDL speeds up the process of stopping the Drama Triangle by depicting where you are stuck in drama triangles in your life. As we have seen in Margo's dream of cancer, if you are playing the Rescuer, Victim, or abuser in your life you will have dream characters giving voice to these roles in your dreams. As you listen to them and neutralize these internal conflicts with wisdom, empathy, and peace, you will stop externalizing your internal dramas as waking life dramas. This is a movement from karma to grace, to which we will now turn.

Exercises

How many ways can you spot the Drama Triangle in your life and in the lives of those around you?

How has the Drama Triangle provided meaning and direction for your life?

How has the Drama Triangle sabotaged your happiness and peace of mind?

10: From Karma to Grace

Tina told me the following dream: "I am a small, young lioness in a cage. There is another lion that someone threw in the cage to eat me! In fact, he starts chewing on my paw! To get him to stop I pretend I am dead and he goes off to sleep. When I think he is totally asleep I start walking around, but he wakes up! We start talking, which is really weird. The lion turns into Ralph, my husband! I tell him that whoever threw him into the cage was trying to kill me. Ralph helps me to escape from the cage, because people are trying to kill us both. He fights and conquers them. Then we evolve from lions to people. Very strange!"

When we interviewed the cage, it told Tina that if it were in charge of her life it would give her the ability to bite her tongue when she's frustrated so she wouldn't get violent like a lion would. She would be more understanding instead of overreacting. A part of her, the other lion, is helping an evil part of her to trap and kill her. The cage advised her not to blow up whenever Ralph antagonized her because it shifted the focus from Ralph being the abuser to Tina's overreaction. It also advised her to get a job so that she would be more independent of Ralph.

The man who put the male lion in the cage told Tina that he is a part of her that wants to keep her under its control by making her think that she can't do anything else than what she is doing. She realized that she is dependent on a critical, abusive part of herself.

Tina said, "What I have heard myself say is that I feel like I am locked up. I feel like I have a pretty life but I can't make certain decisions and I feel trapped. Ralph feels trapped too. He was killing me; he's taken a lot out of my life. But when he realizes that he loves me, he helps both of us to escape. That may be what I really want but there are a lot of obstacles in the way of all that. I still go into rages. That takes away from anything that I do. Ralph is eating my paw. He must still be taking things away from me. He is injuring me. I want to believe that he will save me but he still hurts me.

Tina was a very attractive nurse educator who was ten years into her second marriage and who had a fifteen-year-old daughter. She found herself in a very common predicament: financially secure with a verbally abusive and violent partner who everyone knew was having multiple affairs but that she chose to pretend weren't happening. She was miserable, but too emotionally and financially dependent to leave.

This is a good example of the externalization of a lifelong disowned fear. In this case, Tina was afraid of her anger hurting others. She found herself attracted to men who were strong and verbally abusive like her father was. Because she did not recognize, listen to, and evict the self-abusive part of her father that still lived rent-free inside her thoughts, this pattern was externalized in a way that could not be ignored, by embroiling her in relationships with controlling men. Listening to her dream gave Tina an opportunity to see that she was paying all three roles of the Drama Triangle. As the man and the lion, she was abusing herself. As Ralph, she was taking turns rescuing and abusing herself. As the young lioness, Tina played the Victim. As she listened to what these parts of herself had to say, she began to understand that because she had not addressed her own internal addiction to this Drama Triangle it externalized in her relationship with her husband. However, lifelong addictions to drama are not easily overcome, even with IDL. This is why it is wise to work on an ongoing basis with an IDL Practitioner or other professional who can help you choose useful recommendations from interviews, set meaningful goals, and have an accountability structure to keep you on track. Tina dropped out of therapy and stayed with Ralph. Within two years her daughter was pregnant and the cycle was starting all over, passed down to yet another generation. This is an excellent example of karma.

The word karma comes from the Sanskrit word for action. While it is often used to explain reincarnation, it has a more fundamental use. In Sanskrit, Hinduism, and Buddhism, it can mean "action," or it can mean "divine law." On a personal level, it refers to our sense of responsibility for the consequences of our actions, thoughts, and feelings. Karma is often understood as the externalization in the mirror of our outer circumstances of the consequences of our behavior. We often do not see internal conflicts because they are subjective; we are too close to them to understand them. Such internal conflicts are first objectified in dreams. However, few people have the tools to properly understand these warning signs. If externalization in our dreams does not work to resolve the conflict, as rarely is the case, the depiction of imbalance becomes persistent and shows up as repetitive dreams and nightmares. If we still do not hear, understand, or take responsibility to resolve such conflicts, as few people do, they can externalize in our bodies as illness or pain or in our waking lives as unhealthy relationships, "accidents," or "bad luck." These externalizations are "karmic." Externalization is hardly the only explanation for disease or misfortune; however, it should not be overlooked as an important component in life distress. Few people eliminate externalization of internal conflict as a cause before blaming a microbe, other people, or "fate." To what extent do our intentions, dream actions, and waking actions reverberate across the earth in ways that are incalculable?

To the extent that life is a mirror, our waking relationships reflect back the conditions that exist within ourselves. How is it possible that we can recognize or experience anything that is not already within us? This may have been what Plato had in mind when he explained learning as *amanesis,* or remembering. In our dreams, how we treat others is how we are treating ourselves because the "others" in dreams are actually self-created aspects of ourselves. The golden rule transcends all religions and all times because it states a basic truth about humans: as we treat others so we are treating those aspects of ourselves that they personify. Therefore, it makes no sense to do to others that which we would not have done to us, because we are in fact doing that same action to that part of ourselves that they represent!

It is for this reason that IDL takes all the fun out of aggression. We can no longer be abusive and pretend that we can get away with it. For example, perhaps you dream of a gun battle. Who is shooting at you? When you take the role of the shooter you are likely to recognize that in some way in your life you are shooting at yourself and therefore abusing yourself.

If there were no other reason to practice IDL than to learn this one principle, not as a concept, but as an unavoidable psychic reality, this alone has the potential to transform not only your life, but the violence-loving culture in which we live.

If it is true that how you perceive the actions of others reflects who and what you are, then if you pay attention to what irritates you about others you will learn a lot about yourself.

Many people have difficulty grasping this concept because their experience is that they can successfully lie, cheat, steal, blame others, and generally avoid responsibility for their abusive and disrespectful behavior. For a while they can pretend to be something that they are not and fool others. However, we can only justify self-deception for so long, because part of us always knows when we are not being honest with ourselves. In fact, it may be our reluctance to coming to terms with this reality that is at the psychological root of poor dream recall. Perspectives that embody the truth show up in our dreams, not so much to criticize as to show us the inconsistencies in our lives that create the conflicts that stand between ourselves and a host of qualities that we seek, such as clarity, peace of mind, honesty and self-acceptance.

No one likes to admit that they lied or were irresponsible. Most of us will come up with just about any justification or rationalization to avoid experiencing the loss of face and the feelings of guilt and shame that often accompany such honesty. This is another reason people tend to ignore their dreams. They are afraid they are going to be made to feel guilty by them. Interviewed dream characters are generally much more accepting of our shortcomings than we are of our own. They generally demonstrate healthy alternatives to self-defeating attitudes and behavior. When you accept such assistance you reduce the chance that repressed internal conflicts will show up as physical health problems or mirror themselves back as unhappy relationships.

If karma is basically about seeing yourself wherever you look, then the world is continuously mirroring back to you the consequences of who you recognize yourself to be. This is called the inevitability of projection; a thought, feeling, or action, usually undesirable, is ascribed to someone else when it is actually your own.

If this principle is correct, it is in your best interest to project positive aspects of yourself by looking for the best in others and the world. At the same time, you can take note of the negatives in life and others, approaching them as opportunities for personal growth.

70

If we don't listen to what we are creating within ourselves through our misperceptions, if we continue to misinterpret what is true, misery continues to show up in our lives until we finally see through our self-created delusions. I am reminded of my alcoholic aunt who loved to meet men in bars and was still complaining, after divorcing her sixth drunken husband, about what bad luck she had with men.

There is no reason why misperception has to stop with death. Alcoholics who die are dead alcoholics. Similarly, the Drama Triangle is not going to stop just because you die, any more than it stops because you go to sleep. If you are asleep to your true nature while you are alive there is no reason to believe that you will automatically and miraculously wake up just because you have died. On the contrary, you are likely to fall into an even more unconscious slumber, until you begin dreaming again.

Exercises

What karmic patterns tend to repeat in your life?
How do you keep yourself from healing them?
Identify one that you would like to heal. As you fall sleep tonight, ask for healing of this issue. In the morning write down whatever dreams you remember and ask one or more dream characters the questions from the Interviewing Instructions found in this text or found at DreamYoga.com and IntegralDeepListening.Com.

11: How Your Dreams Create Your Health

Most people give little pause to the time that they spend asleep. Our main concern is that we sleep soundly and awaken refreshed. For most of us that means deep, dreamless unconsciousness, without restlessness, interruption or awareness. As long as such a state remains our priority, any activity that prevents unconsciousness is to be eliminated. As a result, we will sabotage any desire to remember our dreams or heighten our self-awareness while asleep because this will disrupt a basic habit in which we have a deep and long lasting investment. We are under enough stress already; don't we deserve a good night's sleep? Unless you are thoroughly convinced that dream recall a n d dream lucidity contribute in a significant way to your overall health and personal development, no amount of fascination and curiosity about dreaming is likely to make a long-term dent in this basic human desire to sink into oblivion every night.

We know that sleep is regenerative and necessary for health. Do we also know that we must be unconscious for sleep to be healthy? It seems so. A system of toxin removal from the brain has been discovered, and it is much more effective when the brain is inactive in a state of deep sleep. This has in fact been proposed as the adaptational advantage of deep sleep. How is this to be reconciled with the increased brain coherence demonstrated by regular meditators? How is it that some of these meditators can remain conscious in theta (dream) and even delta (deep) sleep?

If health is about being conscious of what hurts us and how to avoid it, then sickness is about being unconscious and sleepwalking our way through life. Waking up, whether becoming more vigilant while asleep or while awake, expands your awareness of yourself. It is about learning how to step outside of who you routinely think that you are and watching yourself go by. The dividends for doing so are enormous.

It is the difference between being a conscious participant in all aspects of life, on the one hand, and, on the other, living a somnambulistic life, a victim of your own unquestioned habitual ways of thinking, feeling, and acting.

While there appear to be clear biological and psychological benefits to sleep, there is also a price to pay for going unconscious. First, your biochemistry controls you. Consider the basic fight or flight physiological reaction to stress. Let's say you are preparing to give an important speech and you are feeling a lot of pressure to do a really good job. You hate public speaking and you would love to avoid giving the presentation, but you know that you can't. You know that you are going to have to put on a brave face and fight your way through it. You go to sleep feeling anxious about how you are going to do. How might this affect your ability to give your speech?

Hans Selye, the brilliant Canadian doctor and researcher, was a pioneer in research on the physical consequences of stress on organisms. He observed and described what he called the General Adaptation Syndrome, the process by which organisms adapt to stress, whether it is an illness, a death, a job loss, or an accident. When we first experience a stress we go into an alarm reaction. A cascade of powerful hormones is pumped out of our endocrine glands to alert and activate our body to deal with danger. Our heart speeds up, our breathing becomes faster and more shallow. Blood flows away from our internal organs and to our skeletal muscles to prepare us to fight or run. Our pupils constrict. If the threat does not go away as a result of all these measures, we next go into an adaptive phase in which we conserve our resources for a drawn-out defense against the attack. Finally, if the threat remains present, we enter the exhaustion phase. At this point new energy is poured into the body in a last-ditch attempt to overcome the challenge; we look like we are rallying when in fact we are making a total expenditure of all our resources in one final effort to turn the tide. If this does not work, we die.

When you have a major life stress, let's say a public speaking phobia, in this case, you can recognize both the initial alarm reaction and the secondary adaptive phase when your anxiety does not go away.

We know that adrenaline, norepinephrine, and other stress hormones collect in the body when the fight or flight response is activated. In waking life, we can metabolize them by fighting or running. However, when you are anticipating a stress like giving a speech you can't do either. A similar situation is created very night when you sleep. During your dreams your central nervous system is paralyzed.

When you go to bed worried, your dreams are more likely to be filled with anxiety-causing themes of inadequacy and failure in an attempt to address your fear.

While you may dream you are fighting or fleeing, that does nothing to neutralize the powerful hormones that are building up in your tissues. Because they are not dissipated they act like battery acid, attacking the weakest link in your body's defense system. Given enough time and enough repeated exposure to these night time assaults on the body, one person may catch some bug because their immune system is depleted; another person may develop arthritis because their auto-immune system goes haywire. Another person may develop high blood pressure and cardiovascular disease, while yet another may develop insomnia or ulcers. Still others may show no effect whatsoever. While genetic predisposition partially determines which system is most likely to collapse beneath the onslaught of these biochemicals, how you handle stress makes an enormous difference in the ability of your body to recover from it.

Fortunately, normal physical activity helps to metabolize and eliminate toxic stress chemicals, which is one reason why regular exercise is so important. If you don't do something physical to metabolize these powerful stress hormones, over time they can destroy your resistance to disease. However, most of us assure ourselves that this is not happening to us. We think about the walking that we do, the exercise that we get, the efforts we make to handle our feelings and responsibilities in ways that don't allow stress hormones to build up in us. Yet we still get sick; our organs break down and we start feeling our age. Is this all due to genes and natural processes of aging, or is there something basic that we are overlooking?

IDL believes that if you want to stay healthy you need to reduce stressful dreams. Reenacting the Drama Triangle in one form or another, in dream after dream, can't be good for your health. You might ask, "How can I be stressed if I am unconscious?"

"How can something affect me that I don't even remember?" Here is an analogy. Every time you eat something it affects you for better or for worse. If it's toxic it will harm your body whether or not, you are aware of its toxicity. Samples of Beethoven's hair showed that he went deaf and eventually died due to lead poisoning, probably from the pewter mugs he drank from during his life.

Similarly, dreams and nightmares that arouse a fight or flight response in you release powerfully corrosive stress chemicals into your body --whether or not you remember any dreams.

Have you ever awakened anxious, irritable, or confused from a deep, dreamless sleep? Something was going on out of your awareness while you slept that created stress. Such events not only leave a physiological residue, making it harder for your body to cope with health risks; they leave a mental and emotional residue that colors your perception and affects your responsiveness, your mood, your mental focus, and your creativity. You don't have to wake up in a foul mood for this process to be taking place. It can be very subtle. Generally, the stress of unhealthy dream experiences undercut your physical, mental, and spiritual development completely out of your awareness. You probably work hard during the day to eat right, exercise, maintain a positive attitude, treat others with respect, not react, and generally be a good person. Could it be that despite all of your excellent efforts that at night while you sleep you are unconsciously undoing, undercutting, and destroying all that you have fought to create during your waking hours? If you are so sure that this is not the case, how do you know?

If you take as a genuine threat something that is only a dream experience, your body cannot tell the difference. For instance, if you dream of public speaking and being embarrassed and humiliated because the audience is laughing at you and walking out, this is your reality. You will respond as if these events happened to you in real life and your body will go into its normal reactions to stress. This may be one reason why psychotherapy is ineffective with many people. They leave the session feeling good, but at night in their dreams they regress into the Drama Triangle and habitual emotional reactivity and mental delusions, thereby undercutting their progress and increasing the likelihood they will wake up in the morning anxious, depressed, or both.

IDL short-circuits this process by re-framing your perception of both waking and dreaming sources of anxiety and depression, so that they need not work themselves out in your dreams. For example, Lorna dreamed that she was in her apartment, up to her waist in water. She was not feeling particularly in danger, although she was worried about all the water damage.

While this dream was somewhat stressful, it just as easily could have never been remembered. It is more like a typical dream than a full-blown nightmare.

However, its recall provided Lorna an opportunity to not only understand important stressors in her life but allowed her to take steps to defuse them before more damage was done.

When the Water was interviewed, it said, "I am all the medications that Lorna is taking for her back pain. I am tranquilizing her because she is afraid of feeling how bad the pain may be. She is being swamped by her fear. If she doesn't stop taking us she is not going to get well. Also, by taking us she does not face up to how her fear keeps her trapped in her apartment. She is afraid to go out because then something else bad might happen to her."

Lorna had been injured in a rear-end collision. Years previously she had sustained a head injury from a freak accident. Now, as before, she was afraid to go outside. By listening to the water in her dream Lorna was able to see that her fear was paralyzing her and causing her to take too much pain medication, which was swamping her with sedation. Armed with this information she told her doctor that she wanted to cut back on the pain meds. The doctor was upset with her, feeling that she was non-compliant and attempting to doctor herself. The doctor was responding as he had been taught, to her pain symptoms, rather than recognizing how her pain medication itself was a defense against a more fundamental problem – her long-term fear. Lorna had to change doctors. When she decreased taking the pain meds she immediately became less groggy and less fearful. She could feel her pain, so she could more accurately tell her doctor where she hurt so he could help her. Clearly, if Lorna had not listened to a relatively insignificant and typical dream she might have made her recovery longer and much more complicated.

Arthur Seligman has described something very similar to Selye's *General Adaptation Syndrome* in his explanation of depression as learned helplessness. He explains how cows, when caught in a bog, will bellow and struggle ferociously to get free. After a while, if their efforts are to no avail, they will struggle less; they have entered the adaptive phase of Selye's General Adaptation Syndrome. If they continue to be sucked down into the bog, they will put up one last heroic struggle before drowning. Seligman noted that cows that are trapped in bogs and yet do not die learn not to struggle; they stop trying to get out, even if they could.

This is adaptation to the ongoing stress of Selye's second stage of his General Adaptation Syndrome. Seligman noted that some of these hopelessly trapped cows that were rescued from bogs by farmers would head right back into the bog again!

Could it be possible that we do something similar in our sleep?

Just like some of us get addicted to horror movies or creepy detective thrillers, could it be that we get addicted to creating stressful dream vignettes that increase our stress and keep us sick? Repetitive, stressful dreams and nightmares appear to point to such a conclusion.

While it is certainly the case that stress can kill you, it is equally the case that a lack of eustress, or healthy stress, will kill you too. You are designed to thrive on reasonable challenges. Avoid them and adaptive vigilance diminishes, leading to system breakdown; pursue them and the energy that you find available to keep yourself healthy expands. If we want to protect our health it is not enough to think good thoughts, take our vitamins and be politically correct. We need to eliminate reactivity in our sleep. In addition, we need to learn how to make sleep as positive an experience as we possibly can. IDL not only teaches us how to recognize and neutralize sleep stress; it amplifies forces in consciousness that actively support health, whether awake or asleep.

Might there be a healthier perspective from which to approach our fears, one that does not cultivate the Drama Triangle or reinforce a mindset of victimization by forces in life we can't control? By practicing IDL in response to her dreams about cancer, Margo could reduce the repeated mental and physiological stressors of experiencing herself persecuted, victimized, and avoiding the real issues through self-rescuing behaviors. Both her dreams and her work with them could begin to function as a form of preventive health care. She learned to listen to wake up calls internally, in her dreams, before they could externalize as crises in relationships, waking events, and her physical health.

In contrast to Margo's own anxiety in her dream, as well as the perspectives of persecution and victimization expressed by the cancer and other people in the room that had cancer, her interview with the woman in the dream who had cancer in her hand was surprising. She said, "I don't think the cancer is going to do anything to me. I'm not going to cut my hand off. I don't believe this is going to be necessary because it is not going to spread."

This is not the comment of a Victim, which the dreamer assumed the lady to be. We can see that the very assumption that victimization is happening tends to create a Rescuer response within us, as it did within Margo.

Consequently, part of the process of outgrowing the Drama Triangle is to move beyond assumptions of Victimization, whether regarding others or ourselves.

But was this wishful thinking? Would following this advice be a foolish avoidance of a real problem? How could Margo tell?

Margo also interviewed this woman's hand. It said, "I know she won't cut me off. I'm a part of her and she will be able to get rid of the cancer. What I like best about being in this dream is that I am connected to this woman and she'll take care of me." Notice that this hand does not see itself as a Victim either. It has confidence that its needs will be fulfilled. This is a trusting part of Margo, one that was not obvious from the dream narrative.

Just because we react to some circumstance we often assume that this is the best or most appropriate way of looking at the situation and responding to it, just as Margo did in the dream by believing her recommendation of amputation was appropriate.

However, decisions based on reactivity are rarely well-thought out and satisfactory in the long run. IDL demonstrates that there always exist authentic perspectives we can access that witness our fear with greater empathy, wisdom, and peace than we ourselves do. Once you take the time to look at your life from the perspective of non-reactive parts of yourself, as Margo did when she became the woman and her hand, empathetic detachment is experienced. This is different from an intellectual gloss on pain. Such experiences can change your perception of your fear, your disease, and your life choices fundamentally. Reactivity loses its reality, necessity, and inevitability. You create space for yourself to breathe and to live well within almost any condition.

The benefit of interviewing a variety of dream characters is that you are provided with a number of perspectives on problems about which you must make decisions. As a result, you are more likely to make decisions that are consensus – representing a greater good for a greater percentage of those perspectives invested in growing your life. To this end, Margo also interviewed the cancer. It said, "My strengths are that I can do anything. Nobody can stop me. I'm very strong, very confident. If I were in charge of Margo's waking life she would be like me. She would have confidence and just do it. It would be helpful for Margo to imagine that she is me when she is overwhelmed or things are a little bit scary. She just needs to be confident." By becoming the cancer Margo was accepting the abuser within herself.

This allowed her to see and accept the strengths that are inherent in those parts of life that scared her. The point of view of cancer allowed Margo to experientially reframe her deepest fears as resources and inner strengths that she had disowned. She could own the confidence of Cancer.

IDL allowed Margo to undo her dream reinforcement of her fears of getting sick and dying. Without the practice of IDL Margo would have continued to send powerful visual and emotional affirmations to her body that she was sick, that she had reason to be afraid, and that she was a helpless Victim. Margo began to see that while this dream seemed to be about victimization and abuse, it not only did not have to be seen that way, it *wasn't* that way.

Margo's experience is the norm for people who practice IDL. The more that you deeply listen to emerging potentials the less inclination you will have to feed scarcity, separation, or ignorance within yourself. You will find yourself outgrowing many of the stuck places in your life. Notice, however, that Margo is still going to get sick and die at some point. Life is much more concerned with *how* you live the life you have than for you to live forever. Margo's interview, just like IDL, are not about eliminating stress, disease, or death, but about outgrowing the factors that destroy the quality of life that you are living, and increasing your ability to be fully alive.

IDL will teach you not to take yourself and the absurdities of the human predicament so seriously. We walk onto the stage of life, play our parts, take our bows, and are gone, melting into all players, all audiences, and all producers. IDL can demonstrate to you that the enlightened states of awareness that you seek coexist with your everyday awareness right now. They are immediately accessible, all the time, if you only know where to look to find them and learn to recognize them. Because these states regularly crop up personified as dream characters and personifications of your life issues that are interviewed by IDL, you are regularly provided with personalized metaphors for advanced states of consciousness. These are not merely visual metaphors; they are experiential openings involving a profound shift in awareness into spaces of vast equanimity, inspiring fearlessness, deep empathy, piercing wisdom, and profound acceptance.

It is wise to treat both your dreams and your life events as wake up calls. There are several reasons for doing so. First, by the testimony of many emerging potentials, that is often what they claim to be. Second, even if this is a comfortable deceit, we can do worse than view all our life events as supportive of our enlightenment. Third, this will allow you to reframe unpleasant, uncomfortable, and painful life events as teaching experiences that will help you to grow if you pay attention to what they are telling you.

You can even interview your physical aches, pains, and ailments using IDL. For example, Barb interviewed her chronic back pain which she associated with the color red. A red cloud filling the room condensed into a Black Boulder:

Black Boulder, please tell me what you look like and what you are doing?
I am about three inches round, wedged in Barb's back… like a pain in the ass!

Black Boulder, what do you like most about yourself? What are your strengths?
I get Barb's attention. She pays attention to me!

Black Boulder, what do you dislike most about yourself?
That I hurt people. I don't like to hurt people but it is the only way to wake Barb up. She needs to wake up to some things!

Black Boulder, if you could change Barb's life any way you wanted, would you? How?
I probably would not change it. It is in her best interest.

Black Boulder, what aspect of Barb do you represent or most closely personify?
Her ability to make herself known.

Black Boulder, if you could live Barb's waking life for her, how would you live it differently?
I would have her eat right, exercise, stop drinking… not stay around Mike so much.

Black Boulder, if you could live Barb's waking life for her today, would you handle her three life issues differently? If so, how?
I would have her lose weight, stop drinking and exercise. She could be a flight attendant again but she may be too old physically. She needs to get her stamina back. It won't be like it was before. She needs to find something where she can

78

lose herself in service to others…maybe the Red Cross. Mike is a very negative influence on her. It is sickening, like her pain. He is making himself sick.

Black Boulder, in what life situations would it be most beneficial for Barb to imagine that she is you and act as you would?

When she needs to be strong and awake to what needs to be changed for her benefit.

Black Boulder, why do you think you are in Barb's life?

To wake her up and get her to move… to focus on what needs to be done.

Black Boulder, how would you score yourself from 0-10 in confidence, empathy, wisdom, acceptance, peace of mind, and witnessing?

confidence 10; empathy 8; wisdom 10; acceptance 10; peace of mind 8; witnessing 9.

Black Boulder, what would it take for Barb to live her life as if she completely manifested these six core characteristics of her authentic self?

She should strike out on her own… take care of her body and soul.

Barb, what have you heard yourself say?

I need to recognize and respect my soul's yearnings. Be true to my soul.

Barb, what have you learned from this experience? How can you use it in your waking life?

To make me wake up and take action.

Notice that from the Boulder's perspective its purpose is to wake her up and that until she does so and takes some action, it is actually in Barb's best interest for it to stay! How many people take such an attitude toward their chronic aches and pains? Notice that the Boulder wants her to make specific, concrete changes in her health and her relationship with Mike. Are these just Barb's goals or do they represent inner perspectives she does not own, or are they some combination of both? The high scores that Boulder gives itself in the six core qualities imply that the boulder is a personification of her potential or prospective self.

Clearly, there are many other questions that can be asked the Black Boulder. This example provides a structure to start an ongoing dialoging process. Sometimes IDL serves to heighten awareness of where and how we are stuck; at other times, as when people design and follow an integral life plan based on those recommendations, IDL becomes a transformational psychospiritual technology. What makes interviewing your dream characters and your life issue personifications a *yoga* is that ongoing process, which is a *disciplined application*.

Hearing inner truth is one thing; using it to motivate you to make changes that are real, lasting, and positive is quite another. In other words, Barb had to decide whether to put the recommendations of her Black Boulder to the test by following its advice in her life. That's the only way that she would be able to know for herself whether IDL actually does what it claims to do. Unfortunately, this is not easy for any of us!

There are reasons why you remain comfortably stuck in your maladaptive and dysfunctional patterns, and they aren't going to go away just because some imaginary Black Boulder comes along and says they should! This is why most people benefit by seeking out an IDL coach or practitioner to help them to create and follow an integral life practice for implementing reasonable recommendations that come out of their interviews.

Carol was worried about a persistent rash that had moved from her legs to her forearms. When she gave a color to her skin irritation it became blood red, as if it had been exposed to oxygen. The red color filled the room and then condensed into a red plastic ball that was hollow and filled with air. It said, "I am most comfortable being in front of Carol. What I like best about myself is that I am an object of entertainment through her bouncing and kicking me around. I like that I have a tough outer surface. If you bounce me I can bounce back. I'm not fragile. I most closely personify Carol's desire to be mobile and to do more. If I were in charge of Carol's life, I would move around more without worry about having the money to do it. I would find more activities to enjoy. Carol is her own worst enemy when she worries. I don't worry. I'm calm and peaceful. If Carol felt the way, I do all the time she would be at peace. She would be able to live her life to its fullest."

Because Red Ball didn't know anything else about why Carol had the irritation of her skin, we decided to ask it directly. The skin irritation said, "I'm aggravating Carol. I like it! I'm a distraction! She focuses on me. I am strong because I have her full attention. I am powerful! I am in control! I keep Carol from going forward. New pursuits cause me to itch. If Carol moves forward I won't exist! By keeping her miserable, I exist and she stays distracted from her fear of growing and changing. I'm trying to keep her from going forward. I most closely personify Carol's hesitation. I would recommend that Carol find another distraction: moving around and enjoying life. If she moved forward I would go away."

Notice that this interview raises all sorts of fascinating questions. Why would a chronic skin rash express itself as a hollow red ball that sees itself as an object of entertainment that is tough and not fragile? Red Ball says that it is a personification of Carol's desire to move around more and to find more activities that she enjoys. Notice that it is calm, peaceful, and doesn't worry, unlike Carol. Therefore, it is not merely a comfortable reflection of Carol's waking perspective. The implication is that Carol can become the red ball when she doesn't want to worry. There is a further implication that Carol's worry has something to do with her persistent rash. When we interviewed the skin irritation it told us that it works to keep Carol safe by not taking on new activities, the very things that Red Ball is recommending that she do. Skin Irritation said, "These new pursuits cause me to itch. If Carol moves forward I won't exist." The Skin Irritation said that it personified Carol's hesitation about trying new things. We then asked Red Ball what it thought about what Skin Irritation said. At this point Red Ball came up with a clear diagnosis for Carol's rash: "Carol is trying to break

80

out or itching to get away from things in her life. Carol taking action will get rid of the rash. If Carol didn't worry the rash would go away."

Now who is to say that any of this is real or accurate? All we are doing is collecting other perspectives and then supporting Carol's experiments in living from those perspectives that are healthy and that hold promise. Notice how the Red Ball sees the rash as a visual metaphor for Carol's issue, "breaking out and itching to get away from things in her life." While this is reminiscent of the types of metaphorical associations to diseases that one finds in the works of Louise Hay, the difference is that these are internally provided rather than externally provided in a "one size fits all" formula that may or may not ring true for you, like symbolic interpretations in dream dictionaries. Red Ball agreed that Carol needed to both take action and work on not worrying. Understanding that her rash might well get worse if she started doing more things, she wanted to see what would happen when she persisted. We developed an integral life practice for Carol that identified specific small ways that she could begin moving forward in her life in ways supported by Red Ball and Skin Irritation. They involved walking daily for exercise, looking for another job, and joining a group of people interested in learning to meditate. As she began to do these things the skin irritation first got worse. Then it started going away. After a month both the rash and the skin irritation were gone.

It is not unusual for our pains and physical health problems to state that they exist to protect us from doing things that are outside our comfort zone. When this is fully understood, we stop blaming ourselves for our problems or seeing them as our adversaries. They simply act as defenses that are the same time wake up calls that these defenses need to be listened to, because they have taken over our lives.

Notice that IDL does not offer miraculous or immediate cures for life's challenges. What it does offer is a pathway to authentic healing, balancing and transformation that is a byproduct of listening to and following the recommendations of both wounded and potential perspectives.

Exercises

Are you genetically predisposed toward any diseases?

If you were to get seriously ill, which bodily systems would be most likely to be first affected?

How likely to do you think it is that the mental-emotional stressors in your life predispose you toward illness?

How do you neutralize the effect of stressful and emotionally upsetting dreams on your physical and mental health?

Interview a dream character of your choice using the interviewing script found in appendix III or interview a life issue or physical symptom using the directions for "interviewing a self-aspect," also found in appendix III.

81

12: Healing Our Social Nightmares

The multiple crises, wake-up calls, and nightmares that the world is currently experiencing are macrocosmic externalizations of our own microcosmic cognitive distortions, avoidance strategies, and addiction to drama. "As above, so below." "As within, so without." "We have met the enemy and he is us."

IDL is a powerful and effective way for you to put to work Gandhi's sage advice: "Be the change you wish to see in the world." Instead of blaming others for our problems or busying ourselves in irrelevant activities to take our minds off our powerlessness in the face of catastrophe, we can turn ourselves into people others want to emulate. The more people who do so the more culture and society will change, from the inside out. New possibilities for healing our planet will open up as we learn to get out of our own way and practice deep listening to ourselves and each other in an integral way.

I am writing at a time in human history when our irresponsibility as a species is catching up with us. I live in the twilight of a golden age of consumption, in which more and more people are becoming skeptical toward government, politics, science, technology, religion, psychology, spirituality and the myth of progress. Capitalism is no longer seen as the goose that laid the golden egg of never-ending increases in standard of living. The dream of unlimited opportunity for those who will only work hard is increasingly seen as a form of social darwinism serving to justify the social position of both the haves and the have-nots. This is because capitalism, by nature, seeks to maximize profits and minimize losses. Corporate managers and owners as part of their mandate and job description, do whatever they can to externalize costs. This is a responsibility to their shareholders. It is precisely this motivation that can be seen behind the continuing support of carbon-based energy, even when there exists overwhelming and conclusive evidence that the earth, its habitats, species, and humans cannot maintain current patters of exploitation and consumption. Because social and environmental costs are rarely tied to their industrial sources, there is an illusion of profit when in fact costs are astronomical and rising. Consequently, mankind's dream of unlimited progress is quickly turning into a nightmare that is always caused by the other guy.

Like corporations, individuals are in the business of externalizing costs. If I can get you to take responsibility for my mess, then I don't have to deal with it. All of us play some version of "the dog ate my homework." It's the terrorists, immigrants, politicians, capitalists, communists, socialists... We externalize the costs of continuing to eat in ways that destroy our planet. We continue to eat animals even though doing so contributes more to global warming than automobile emissions and airplanes through the combined devastation of cropland, coral reefs, and river ecosystems while the emissions of livestock, including 1.5 billion cattle, produce methane, which is twenty times more potent than carbon dioxide in its ability to warm the planet.[14]

Disowning dreaming is another common and fundamental form of externalizing costs. This may be done by assuming dreams are objective and real experiences and therefore something we are not responsible for. It may also be done by relying on a book, psychic, or therapist to tell us what they mean. It may be done by simply not remembering them, under the theory that we won't be hurt by what we are unaware of.

Unfortunately, at least some dreams do not work like that. Instead, they become louder and louder until they become nightmares or externalize like Carol's rash did. We can think of the global dream of mankind in a similar fashion. How many news stories had there been about global warming in the years and months prior to Katrina? How many news stories and intelligence reports about terrorist attacks were published prior to 9/11? How many terrorist attacks were there prior to 9/11? If we do not listen to wake-up calls they continue to get louder and louder.

Mankind, however, is by far the most adaptable species to ever evolve on this planet. Once he fully wakes up to how he is fouling his own nest, he will adjust accordingly. IDL has a role to play in this awakening because it is a practice of learning to answer wake-up calls before they reach drastic proportions.

You can do this by treating waking issues and nightmares, like 9/11, as dreams and interview the characters in them as if they were aspects of your own personal dream, as I did with the following excerpts. You will create your own personal and unique version of the same world events, so what follows is not what you would find if you interviewed the same characters. In fact, I invite you to interview several characters from the following cultural nightmare and find out what it says to you and about you.

I am watching first one, then another huge jet full of passengers crash into the New York World Trade Center in huge fireballs, then collapsing, killing thousands, including the terrorists. The Pentagon is also horribly attacked by a jet bomb. Fires rage. People are in shock, then grieving, then outraged. President Bush prepares the country for war.

Here is some of what I had to say as the "dreamer" of this waking dream:
"I really dislike myself a lot for letting this happen to me. How could I have been so blind? Why didn't I see this coming? I really don't like that I am watching because it feels so passive, so helpless! I feel so powerless just watching! When the Towers were stabbed by those jet bombs I felt a huge part of myself die! I hate the terrorists that they would do such a thing! I struggle to separate the human beings from their actions. I know that I am not actually hating the terrorists but

---

14 *Livestock's Long Shadow,* Food and Agricultural Organization of the United Nations.

their thoughts, actions, and feelings. But it feels like I am hating the terrorists themselves because I am having trouble separating who they are from what they do, think, and feel. I like President Bush because I respect the significance and importance of the role of president at a time like this. I don't like him a lot because I don't trust that he or his advisers have the vision to see past their anger and will simply create more terrorism through their reactivity.

I don't understand how this war can be won. I think it is a war that everyone has to agree not to fight, because I see only losers in this war. What I dislike most about being in this dream is the feeling of powerlessness." Here is some of what I had to say as the "Towers:" "I am very, very, angry that you let me be attacked and destroyed! You deserve to be angry at yourself! You were neglectful and irresponsible, so complacent and lazy that you ignored not only my safety but ignored countless warnings that we were in danger!

Your passivity is disgusting. Ignoring the injustices in the world won't make them go away! It just makes them bigger when they do finally happen. War sounds like a good idea. What do we have to lose? We'll show people they can't treat us like this!"

Next, we hear from the "Planes:" "We hate Dream Self for being so passive and not taking care of us. He wants the power and the freedom we give him but he is unwilling to exercise the responsibility that we require. He is like a baby playing with matches around gasoline! He's just blown up his house and charred himself! What I dislike most about being in this dream is being a helpless Victim and the means to the destruction of thousands."

Here is some of what I had to say as the "Fireballs:" "I don't care about the NYWTC or the Pentagon at all, except that they become fuel for me to exalt myself in my glory. The planes and passengers are fuel. The crash allows me to live, so I love it. I love myself! I love to burn! The terrorists allowed me to express myself, to make my glorious nature known to all. So I like them. Other than living fully, I really don't care. What I like most about being in this dream is being free, powerful, and fully alive!! What I dislike most about being in this dream is that it had to end. I would have liked to have burned forever."

Here is some of what I had to say as the "Terrorists:" "We have only contempt for Dream Self. He is not worth hating or even disliking. We like a lot that he is watching, because he is learning of his powerlessness against us, his complacency. He is dreaming his dream of safety and security while he parasitically lives off of us, robbing our lands of their resources, occupying our holy places, supporting those who commit terrorist acts against our women and children. If we have to die, he will die too. But in our deaths the glory and superiority of Islam will shine. They are sleeping cowards; we are courageous holy warriors who put our faith above our comfort and our lives, so unlike what these swine do. Our deaths, the deaths of these symbols of American arrogance, the deaths of all these accomplices to the murder of our cultures, bring glory to us and our cause."

"We hate these buildings for what they symbolize - the arrogant attempt to dominate our land, our culture, our faith. The planes we like a lot as instruments of our punishment. We like the passengers because we can make a greater statement through their terror and helpless deaths. We dislike them as American taxpayers who support the abuse of our culture. We love the carnage, horror, grief, and even the outrage, because now they know exactly how we feel and we have felt for decades now, humiliated by their arrogance and conceit. What we like most about being in this dream is waking Dream Self and America up to us. Making them realize that they not only cannot ignore us, that they can't just take us seriously. By our deaths we are forcing them to recognize, address, and respect our legitimate needs. So our deaths are good. War is good, because we will triumph. The deaths of all these people is absolutely necessary."

Here is what "Bush" said: "I put on a brave face, but deep down I don't know if I have what it takes to handle this one. I very much want to go to war, because it gives me an agenda around which I can unite the people. I was going to have trouble otherwise. But I just don't know about this war. I want to get revenge, but I am not sure who to attack and I don't see an exit strategy. I feel pretty uneasy about this.... What I like most about being in this dream is having a chance to give hope and prove that I'm a capable leader. What I dislike most about being in this dream is that I'm out of my depth. What I dislike is that I really don't know what to do and that this is going to make me look powerless and incapable if I'm not careful."

I n *Dream Sociometry*, the dreamwork methodology that produced the above interviews, we also give voice to the part of ourselves that creates the dream in the first place, called "Dream Consciousness." In this instance, Dream Consciousness would be the group cultural consciousness that created the world nightmare of 9/11. When it was interviewed, it said, "I really hated having to create this drama.

I hate that Dream Self was so fast asleep, so complacent, that I had to kick him hard in the ass to wake him up. I had to not just make him mad, but angry. It's a risk I'm taking, because he could use his anger to turn me off. He could use his anger to hurt himself. But if I don't wake him up, he'll fall even deeper asleep. Then I will have to kick him even harder to wake him up. So now I've hurt him. But I've got his attention. Now that he's alert, is he going to listen, or just stay angry? I hate that I have been forced to hurt my own creations. But it is time to wake up or die. If he does not wake up, then what good am I? Death is better than the selfish insolence of somnambulism.

What I like most about creating this dream is my willingness to take great risks in order to create a greater good. My hope is that Joseph will come to respect the needs of ALL parts of himself instead of wasting his life ignoring the legitimate needs of parts of himself and therefore stay at war with himself. What I dislike most about creating this dream is the pain, fear, and anger it has caused.

Many interviewed emerging potentials recommend meditation. The Terrorists

85

recommended that I "listen to the disenfranchised within myself."

There are many provocative and insightful comments in such an interview. But perhaps the most important thing to notice is how clear, distinct, and autonomous the various perspectives are while coexisting within one identity. Notice also that the basic message is to take responsibility for ALL of one's experience, good, bad, and ugly. There is something to learn about yourself in everyone and everything, particularly in those people and events that upset you the most. The more that you and I take responsibility for what we have done to our relationships and our planet, and develop empathy with other perspectives that create our reality, the more effective will be our efforts to awaken within our life dream. We cannot wait for government to show leadership on this issue. In fact, it has done the exact opposite. Instead of waking up, it fell more deeply into a Drama Triangle of blaming others (terrorists) and used this as justification to fight ward of aggression and destroy citizen rights to privacy. You cannot wait for others to evolve out of the Drama Triangle. You have to decide you are sick of it and accept responsibility to practice IDL for yourself, in your own personal and business relationships. It's time. The world needs you.

Exercises

Pick a nightmarish life event and interview characters in it like I did. What do you discover about yourself?

13: Using IDL to Support Your Growth Toward Wholeness

Once upon a time, in a far away kingdom, a king sat on his throne, on a small island in the middle of his realm. He was holding audience before his subjects. The king had his leg up on a stool, and it was wrapped in a white plaster cast; he had apparently broken it. Unknown to the king and his subjects, archers had moored a boat behind and had crept up on the event. They drew their bows and announced that they were holding the king for ransom. He had to either surrender all of his gold or they would kill him.

The problem was, unknown to the archers or the citizens of the realm, several generations previously, when the country was under siege, all the gold of the kingdom had disappeared. The king had no ransom to pay; he didn't know what to tell the archers. If he said the gold was gone, it would expose him as powerless and a fraud, and he would lose his throne; if he lied and said he had the gold when he did not he would be found out to be a liar.

In the silent suspense of the moment, as everyone waited for the king's answer, someone called out, "Look! Look at the king's cast!"

Everyone strained to look at the king's white plaster cast on his outstretched broken leg. The white plaster was scratched below the knee, and in the torchlight there was the unmistakable glint of gold!

The king was as amazed as the others. He didn't know what to make of this strange sight. As he pondered, it slowly dawned on him what had taken place. Slowly, the king told his captors and subjects the story.

Years ago, during the reign of his grandfather, the kingdom had been threatened by invasion. Fearing the loss of the kingdom's treasure, his grandfather had all of the precious wealth of the kingdom taken to the royal foundry. There it was fashioned into all sorts of common items: spoons, bowls, plates, and door latches, covered with a natural glaze, and distributed throughout the homes of the kingdom for safety! All these years he and his father before him had ruled as if they possessed the wealth that validated power and authority when they did not! Instead, it was lying hidden, safely concealed in the humble homes of all his subjects!

There was stunned silence. The archers were angry. No wealth to steal! The subjects were confused. "Why have this man be king?

He has no wealth, and therefore no power!" But slowly all realized that the wealth was everywhere, more than any of them could want, free for the taking! Wealth was no longer an issue! The archers put down their bows, because there was no longer any wealth to steal. The people now looked at the king simply as a man who ruled them. Had he been just? Had he listened? Had he protected them? They agreed that he had. And because of this, they realized that they wanted him to continue to be their king. He could rule because of who he was, not because of what they thought he had. They celebrated their new wealth and their king into the night.

I had this dream when I was about twenty-three and living in Charlottesville, Virginia, sleeping on a couch in an apartment. Years later, when I learned to interview dream characters, the king told me he was a personification of my waking identity, which rules by custom and habit much more than by any earned right. I knew that in this regard I was something of a sham in the power I wielded over the rest of myself, and therefore was living something of a lie. I was pretending to be much more powerful and in control of myself and my life than I was! Through this dream I came to realize that the sacred wealth that I sought and that gave meaning and purpose to my life was everywhere around me, hidden just beneath the surface in the secular and mundane of my everyday life. My job was to rule myself honorably through the quality of my character rather than through power and control. My understanding of what it meant to be a responsible world citizen expanded.

This dream "fable" was important for me at that time and still is. It taught me to look for the sacred in the most mundane aspects of life, myself, and others. I learned from it that the self only rules by a combination of its power and the consent of the physical, mental, and emotional society that it governs and represents. Real power is actually distributed throughout consciousness, in the mundane moments and experiences of life, hidden just below the surface. It is in letting go of dishonest claims to power that waking identity can claim real authority, based on the earned respect of the intrasocial community that it governs.

This moves us from a karmic, dishonest, and fear-based relationship with our internal constituency to a more graceful, honest, and trusting relationship with ourselves.

For most of us, growth requires shoulders to lean on. Others not only provide models for behaviors that teach us lessons, they provide mirrors of our own development. They provide us with external sources of objectivity. While external sources of support are very important, they can present problems. For example, you can become so committed to a path that you stop listening to your own life compass. This is what happens when one becomes a True Believer in a religion, an economic system, a nation, or a philosophy of life. When you become invested not only in following but in defending someone else's definition of truth, that religion or group or path or teacher becomes more important than being true to your most central and authentic being. This is a recipe for disaster. People routinely make this error in choosing mates as well. Have you? Have you ever deluded yourself into believing that you have found your soul mate when you have only unfairly projected all your unrealistic expectations and idealized distortions onto another person? In addition, while external sources of truth can indeed provide you with inspiration, that spark soon fades, leaving you perplexed as to how something that felt so good, so right, so genuine, could vanish so completely.

Because dreams, feelings, and physical symptoms are universal, there is nothing about IDL that conflicts with external sources of objectivity. It is meant to enhance the path that you are already on rather than supplant it. If you are a Mormon, Hindu Vedantist, scientific materialist, CEO, Zen meditator, humanistic therapist, accountant, health care professional, Catholic, or Muslim, IDL is designed to strengthen your journey on your path. You need to keep doing what already works in your life. IDL encourages you to use whatever teachers, priests, scriptures, groups, and practices that you are already comfortable with. Anything and everything can and should be approached as an aid to your development because we all need external sources of objectivity.

One of my clients who had worked with IDL for over three years was a Jehovah's Witness. I watched her grow in confidence, acceptance, wisdom, empathy, and inner peace within the context of her culture and her value system. Beware of those who want to shape you into their image! Take root exactly where you are and flourish, letting your light and your unique gifts awaken the best within those around you.

If you want change in your life you have to ask yourself, "Is this a change my life compass wants? How do I know? Have I interviewed emerging potentials? Or have I simply internalized external sources of authority as "conscience," "intuition," "God's will," "soul purpose," "karma," "soul," "spirit," or "higher self," and supposed that was the same as my life compass? Because life itself accepts you completely and does not die, it has no need to change. While it may support you in changes that you make, it is presumptuous to assume that you are following your life compass unless you ask prospective dream characters and personifications of your life issues and they say that you are.

A core component of waking up involves your ability to stand back and witness yourself and the dream of your life. This ability is fundamental to confidence, empathy, wisdom, acceptance, and inner peace. Every time that you identify with an emerging potential you are dying to your habitual waking orientation and vantage point. You are choosing instead to witness yourself from the perspective of whatever part of yourself is personified as a lunchbox, a garden lizard, a UFO, or the Grand Canyon. When you experience yourself from one of these perspectives you are cultivating those aspects of the witness that it personifies. The importance of this cannot be overestimated.

This ability to witness came to Rita in the form of a saguaro cactus. It said, "Rita doesn't have to be in control.

She can still be herself. She is strong enough to stand like me, a saguaro cactus, and not let these things interfere or cause problems. She can be empathizing with Larry with what he is going through without being involved and pricked by it."

"Nothing bothers me because I have my barbs to protect me from people injuring me or even touching me. I have collapsible barbs that will go away when I want people to touch me but are there when I don't want to be touched. I prefer to be in the corner of the yard because it feels safer, not exposed from all sides. My most tender side is not exposed except when I want it to be. I can swivel when I am ready to have someone touch me on my tender side. Rita is already living her life like I am; she just doesn't fully realize it yet!"

These comments by Rita's "saguaro" muse helped her to own her strength, her ability to protect herself, yet be vulnerable when she so chose.

The fact that Rita had this dream implies that these awarenesses were already being born within her; what IDL did was simply speed up that birthing process by making her waking self a conscious supporter of that process.

IDL uses two sanghas, or spiritual communities, to provide you with the objectivity you need to develop the ability to witness yourself. The first is your internal Sangha of interviewed subjective sources of objectivity. It is made up of those dream characters and personifications of your life issues that have demonstrated by the quality of their guidance and their self-ratings that they personify transpersonal perspectives. They are consulted about life decisions related to their area of expertise. The second is your external or social Sangha, comprised of those external sources of objectivity who share with you a desire to listen to emerging potentials that personify both their wounds and their potentials and to apply those recommendations that make sense in their waking lives. These are more narrowly your brothers and sisters in the IDL community, but more broadly all people, animals, plants and beings everywhere. This is because everything mirrors back to you your potential to live, if you cultivate eyes to see it.

Wherever you are, whatever you do, your world mirrors back to you the truth of your nature and points the way to expressing the uniqueness of your gifts to the world. Your external Sangha becomes your peer group for the practice of IDL. If you have some issue or concern, they are there to assist you. If you interview them, they will tell you what you need to know.

The external support group that shares with you a commitment to the "yoga" of deep listening is called your IDL Sangha. It may or may not be led by a person trained in IDL, called a practitioner. IDL provides a vehicle for those who seek to support others in their efforts to align their lives with a life agenda that transcends and includes that of their waking sense of who they are.

The structure of an IDL Sangha, also known as an "Integral Salon," which may meet weekly, bi-weekly, or monthly in person, by teleconference, or on line, is simple. If there is no IDL Practitioner or coach, members can select a leader or rotate that position. The leader reads or shares a statement of purpose which explains what a IDL Sangha is and the order of the meeting. A statement of purpose can be found in Appendix I. A topic for the evening can be chosen and announced in advance.

After discussion, the group leader can lead the group through an interview associated with the topic, or she can ask who has a dream or life issue that they would like to share as a demonstration interview. The set of interviewing instructions in the appendices are used to direct the questioning. This generally takes about half an hour. A transcript of the session is made, both to read back to the person being interviewed and to give to them so that they may have a copy of the interview to read over, particularly before sleep.

Making a transcript of the interview satisfies several functions. When people are in role they are not expected to think about or remember what they say, because that tends to take them out of role. When a transcript is created, they can read what occurred. Secondly, reading back what was said as statements that the dreamer is making about themselves supports the acceptance and internalization of the characteristics of the role they assumed.

Thirdly, it provides another source of inspiration and direction for the group as a whole. My preference is to type on a laptop the answers to the questions that I ask characters. I then email a copy of their work to them.

Finally, other Sangha members share with the group how the comments of the interviewed emerging potential resonates for them in their lives and how they themselves could benefit from using it in the coming week.

The purpose of the IDL Sangha, in addition to putting participants in touch with powerful and inspirational sources of practical direction, is to provide listeners with the opportunity to be inspired and directed by the words of those characters that are given voice. If participants think they know what the dream means, they may ask the characters for their opinion regarding that interpretation. They may also ask characters personal questions about their own lives if they so desire. The group may also ask characters questions about the growth and development of the Sangha itself.

Your emerging potentials are always there for you, to provide you with the support you need when you need it, whether the world is there for you or not. Rebecca interviewed a group character, People in a Car. It told her, "This is our point of rejuvenation. It's like our Sangha. Rebecca has the capability to be with us. She just needs to meditate. The dilemma is that physically she thinks she needs to be different than she is. She doesn't.

She can do this but it's not the way she thinks. It's through her ability to meditate and connect on that level.

We don't represent a physical group that she has to join. She has been struggling with joining Unity or AA to have some connection, but she needs to realize that the connection is there within her. She's doing good. She's been meditating. We are here to confirm that she is doing well and we are here at any moment. We are glad that she is where she is. She can best make use of us by connecting with us throughout the day. We are her spiritual family; we are her guides. We are here to assist her. All she has to do is think in a brief moment about us and we are there."

"If she experienced herself as inside the car and with us whenever she meditates she will realize she doesn't need to join anything at this time. If she calls on us we will bring her a sense of peace and that everything is good. It's not going to be a hard journey. The job thing is not going to be a big deal. She's very capable. The issue is that she didn't feel that she is connected and that she needs to join groups. She doesn't. She will attract to herself like-minded individuals. We are angels and we can fly! We are here for her. She needs to remember that we are here and to call on us whenever she wants to. It's not about help but about her being a special being and that she is not alone. We don't see Rebecca as alone and we don't want her to feel alone either. She will know that everything is OK and that she is where she needs to be. The timing on everything is perfect."

Rebecca said, "What I heard myself say that I don't need to join anything. It's a time of replenishing. A big weight is lifted from me by coming back here. The issue with my family is that they are operating from their own consciousness. I can't judge them but I can speak my truth, and I am. I need to be a little more patient with my mother and allow her own journey. This group is there for me daily, always. I just need to call on them. It's just going to get better. The job thing will unfold. Not just do something, just to do something! This (difficult) time is temporary if I look at the whole picture. I need to learn to enjoy things because life changes so quickly."

Your path through the swamps of life shows itself to you everywhere, even in your nightmares. James shared the following dream: "I am sitting on a hard wood floor. All around me in this room are cold stone walls going up about thirty feet. Three is no visible light source. It's dim. I am sitting in a meditation posture meditating.

I see the figure of a man, sinewy, dark face, pointed, with very defined features. It is not the face of a man, more the face of a monster. It scares me. Then all of a sudden he's levitating in front of me and he communicates with me! I instantly realize that this is my guru, my spiritual teacher. I realize I have nothing to fear. I realize this entity is going to take me to the ever-loving bliss of God.

Slowly I start to levitate with him, but not with my body. It's almost as if my essence is coming up. I feel this raw ecstatic joy, love, and bliss. I can't even describe how it feels! It's a feeling of oneness with the universe! I know I am stepping out of dualism and that my time is up in material creation and that I am starting to merge with the infinite."

The guru said to James, "I like my face. I dislike that my face scares you but you need to see that which is beneath appearances. I could have come as anything. I chose this body to teach. I'm here to help you reconnect with the infinite, with self-realization. James has desire in his heart and his soul to find the truth. He has desire to escape limitations that he places on himself. In his heart he called to me so I have come to him. I go about levitating because I am one with the universe. I can be anywhere, anything, at any time. I can be a man floating in the air."

"I most closely personify James' higher self. He needs to see his higher self as a monster because that's how he wants to see me in the moment. He's still afraid of the future, he's still afraid of letting go. So in his fear he creates a monster. My greatest strengths are my oneness with everything, my total realization and understanding of the universe. The reason why I am in this dream is to show James that there is hope, that this does not have to be done alone, and that in his strivings he should not do everything alone, that he has support, that he is always loved, forever, and that connection is never broken."

"If I were in charge of James' life I wouldn't change it. He's doing what he needs to do right now. He changed some things recently and it was exactly what he needed to do. Regarding money, his faith in spirit is strong but his patience is weak. He has little patience. He is learning to experience and have patience and realize that what he desires will come to him when he needs it to.

He must continue to do what he is doing, having faith and being patient, not letting anxiety overcome his reason. Let it out, let it go, and give it away. He is going to be a good father, but he knows that.

Regarding being a single father, this situation will take care of itself. Nothing is needed to do, just to be and to go with it."

"James will benefit from identifying with me by realizing that I am always here, that he will grow into me, and he will be one. He just needs to keep smiling and laughing. Play a little more! His lower self has been neglected a little. Follow his heart! Regarding IDL, it's a wonderful thing for him to learn. He will learn higher forms of meditation and self-realization later in life, but his desire to help others will lead him into teaching other things that will help them know themselves."

Exercises

Stop reading now and see how long you can go without thinking. The average adult can go no more than 60 seconds without having a thought. How long can you go?

In IDL, you will meet emerging potentials that do not think. They are pure witness. As you learn to become them, they will teach you how to meditate.

14: What Students Say About IDL

Students of IDL anywhere in the world can read texts that teach the method, answer questions about what they read, practice interviewing themselves and others, and apply interview recommendations, and earn a certificate as an "IDL Coach." Or, they can take a series of seminars to learn the method. After each interview, students respond to the following series of questions.

What do you think that you (or your interviewee) most got out of the interview?

If you interviewed someone else, how can you follow up to see how he/she is applying his or her experience?

What went well?

Was there any place where you or the interview subject was confused?

What have you learned from the experience of interviewing this person?

What have you learned about IDL?

What have you learned about yourself?

Here are some examples of the types of responses to these questions that students have sent regarding their adventure with IDL:

"I have learned that one dream can personify both your darkest and lightest sides at once. It amazes me how the characters in the dream can be present to show you exactly what you need to hear, exactly when you need to hear it. They bring it up front and in your face! It really illustrates how we each have these opposite qualities within us and that they are perfect for us. It helps me not to judge people so much. It also helps me to learn something more about the person I interview. Even my mother, who I know very well! Each time I interview I learn a better way and gain more confidence in my questions."

"What I have learned about IDL is how it ties in with our core selves, how it bypasses all of the daily B.S. and personas we establish to get us down to what is truly who we are. That is a special thing; it is a gift to be able to access what is divinely ours. It is also a gift for me to be able to help someone in this way. I never realized this before. It is beautiful to interview someone and have them look at you like you answered questions that have been haunting them for a lifetime! Of course, I haven't answered any of their questions – I've just helped them to access their own truth."

"And now they finally see the light and feel more confident on their path, or maybe you helped to show them their path when they were so lost. I want to do this with people daily! It shows me one example of the power to heal ourselves. I have always said that 'You have the power to heal yourself." I am only a vessel for that knowledge. I am here to show you the path, and support you on your journey.' I learned that IDL is something that I really enjoy and want to use in my life and in others' lives."

94

"I have learned that I really can hold that space with someone and put in my ideas. I learned that I am a better listener than I thought! I benefits are huge in listening to the messages that we constantly get every day, but shrug off like they are not important. I have learned h listen to myself as well as others."

"I think that Rachael really got a lot out of this experience, so much cannot put words on it so well. I think that she got the opportunit some things and felt that she had a safe place to do it. I learned Rachael from this interview. There is a lot more going on than the eye learned how much she really loves herself! What I learned about amazingly it works with people who have the desire to help themsel much more powerful! What I learned about myself is that I resonate w her stuff and this helped me to think about things as well!

"I think my student most got out of the interview that inner aspects of be very interesting, wise, and loving, and provide her with what she ne journey each step of the way.
I can follow-up to see how she is applying her experience by asking h self-loving aspect is doing.
It all went well I thought, as she easily had access to listening to her cl learned that I would really like to interview the cat, too, and that IDL is its fun and insight! I have learned that I like interviewing and I like tal Vicki. I have learned that there is a self-love aspect similar to this chara my own soul and that I am starting to use my Sangha members. I reme become my microphone when I had to share my experiences with all th strangers last Friday and everything went well! At least I think it did!"
"The lady that I interviewed had been somewhat stressed about her hus been complaining about the time she spends at school. She realized thr listening to her emerging potentials that she has to pay more attention t marriage without giving up who she is and who she is trying to become wants to do another interview and she said that next time she wants to i either her cousin or the baby cribs. She went into character like it was s nature! Although I'm not married or in a relationship at this time, I lear valuable lesson based on her life issues and her character's realizations she needs to do to create unity in her marriage. What I learned about ID just keeps getting better and better."
"I think that Marcy got the opportunity to practice standing aside and be witness. I think she had a hard time but that is good in that it showed he does it and what she needs to do to improve that. I think it is a great gai to be able to stand aside and witness sometimes. Also, I think that she b from seeing that these issues are still lingering somewhere inside of her

e can clear them out a little more. I will ask her in class or on the computer when I talk to her there. I will ask her if she noticed anything different within herself or her daily life. This dream seems important to her so maybe another one we could interview more characters for more insight and further growth. It made sense that it was difficult for Marcy to be the character of her sister since she knows her and has feelings for her.

Interviewing Marcy has given me more of an insight about how awful it is to torture your younger siblings.

As off the subject as that may be, that is what I think stands out for me about what she talked about and how she is still hurting from those seemingly significant things. I have learned that IDL is about nurturing parts of us that need lovin' too!

Not about fixing everything and being this perfect being, but about giving all of the parts of us attention too so that these things stop acting up in our waking lives. Just like a child who feels that they are not getting adequate attention in the moment, will be naughty until they get what they need. Wow! That really helps me to understand my son more. When he gets a little naughty, I can go over and spend some time, just us, and then he is not naughty anymore! If every parent knew that!"

"I learned that I am wasting my time expecting to fix every little aspect of myself to perfection. Even thinking that would be possible is unreal! But like we talked about, I am just learning to nurture every part of myself more. Let it have its time to speak to me in its own way and get messages to me, as it should. I think I learned more about self-respect. How respectful is it to ignore any part of me and to assume that I need to change or 'fix' it when I do get in touch with it? I need to respect me by listening to me as I would desire others to listen to my waking me."

"I have learned to remember that people see good things in me that I know are there, and I have learned to believe it myself. I think June realized that she does have some awesome gifts that she is afraid to bring out and that she has an extensive support "committee" or Sangha within her who are very willing to help her get through her fear. I see her in class and we have agreed to continue to get together. She was able to get into role and stay there fairly easily. I think she was very aware of what she is doing subconsciously to keep her gifts hidden inside because of some very strong past life fears. I was glad that she felt comfortable enough with me to want to tell me about her family and things that have happened to her in her past. I like the simple, step by step process that leads gently to healing or transformation. It is not an overly complicated process."

"This was the first time I had the opportunity to work with a sensation...this feeling of exhilaration. It is also the first time I worked with someone that has the challenge of a disability.

Don was hit by a car when he was two years old, his left arm is completely

96

paralyzed and twisted. I was humbled by the experience and felt honored to share IDL with Don. How beautiful it was to see a person that feels so broken find a part of themselves that is completely whole!

He found a part of his inner self that is immune to judgment, a part of the soul that has complete courage and unconditional love! This part of Don sees limitations as being abstract. I think that is something we all long for...we search for purpose that is beyond time and space. I think for a short moment, Don realized that his soul is not his body, his soul is not a disabled Man, or a Lover, or a lonesome Father...he realized that there is a part of him that is infinite bliss."

"This interview with Don really encouraged me to put forth my best effort, to continue sharing with each person that I come into contact with. I hope that Don will make time for IDL. I let him know that I would be honored to work with him some more if he has the desire to do so."

"My student realized she was expecting her father to make a change in his attitude about what had happened, then realized that his behavior is out of her control. I have learned that regardless of how much the problems of other family members and/or others can affect us, to make sure that we don't make their problems ours -- feel and help, but not make the problems ours. With each interview, I am learning that by interviewing the dream characters, just how profoundly we can understand our waking behavior and reactions to situations that at times we don't see or realize in waking life. I have learned from the interview that I want to become more aware of my reactions to the life challenges that happen to others and notice when I am taking it on so that it doesn't interfere with my life or health. In the past, I would take on others' problems and challenges as if they were my own. In fact, I still do sometimes, and I want to keep an eye on that."

"I think by doing this interview I have learned a lot about appreciating people for who they are and not what they have to offer. Vicki received a lot of validation from other parts of herself and now has a clearer recognition of her many gifts. Her recall of the dream seemed to fit her waking reality.

It seems as if she's closer to acceptance of her many and different talents. Every character was in line with her life issues. I've gained a deeper understanding of Vicki's struggle with her talents. I have learned that IDL is a very special tool for self-exploration. I've learned to see how far I've come in my own growth and acceptance."

Exercises

What priorities of your own emerging potentials do you need to emphasize more in your life?

How would your life be different if you had a means of being at peace with wh[15]atever issues were in your life at the time?

Conclusion

What makes IDL so effective is its differentiation of your life compass, as the perspectives of interviewed dream characters and personifications, particularly those that score higher than you do in the six core qualities that are associated with emerging potentials and awakening, from conscience, intuition, "higher self," and other non-operationally defined definitions of inner guidance. In addition, its effectiveness can be validated by anyone: simply define your interview recommendations in operational terms, follow them, and see what happens in your life. Whether the world is ready for such an approach is another matter. Most of us have great difficulty suspending their assumptions about what is good, real, and true, a step that is important if we are to get out of the way and allow largely autonomous perspectives to be heard. We also rebel against the idea of sharing power with imaginary and mundane objects, characters, and images. In addition, we often resist applying the recommendations we receive from interviews in our lives, even when we regard them important, necessary, and transformational. We generally prefer to keep doing things pretty much the way we always have. Consequently, if IDL does not speak to you, know that you are in the vast majority. Broadening our perceptual preferences seems to be easier when it comes from others, through a course, the internet, or just about in any form other than from dreams and imaginary images that seem both irrational and irrelevant. However, wake-up calls, whether in the form of health problems, nightmares, challenging relationships, or work are a staple of life; therefore tools to more effectively listen to those wake-up calls and to heed them earlier, like IDL, can bring huge dividends.

Appendix I: Statement of Intent

Intention generates meaning and focuses both attention and effort. The IDL Statement of Intent is a summary of many of the salient concepts that describe IDL. This statement can be repeated to remind oneself of why they are alive, where they are going, and what they are attempting to accomplish today. Elaborations on these concepts are found in different texts describing IDL.

I am asleep, dreaming, sleepwalking,
lost in the drama of my life script,
stuck in the perceptual reality of my
physical, mental, cultural and social filters.
I am here to wake up.
I do so as I ask, "Is this a dream?"
see everything as a wake-up call,
reframe my cognitive distortions,
and act on my priorities and those of my life compass today
moving me from delusion and mental fuzziness
to clarity and thence to
luminosity, cosmic humor, and abundance.

I am addicted to the past and future,
to my feelings, thoughts and sense of self.
I move from distress, anxiety and depression
into the here and now
as I name the contents of my mind,
stop monkeying around in the five trees
(thoughts, feelings, imagery, sensations, and states),
and become the seven octaves of the round of my breath,
moving me from personalization to
cosmic humor, abundance, and luminosity.

I have lost my way.
I find and follow my life compass
as I amplify my sense of inner peace and
remember, become, and deeply listen to emerging potentials,
applying their recommendations with triangulation in my daily life,
integrating my inner and outer worlds
and moving me from fear-based scarcity to
trust-based abundance, luminosity, and cosmic humor.

Appendix II: IDL Life Issue Interviewing Protocol

Joseph Dillard, LCSW, Ph.D.

What are three fundamental life issues that you are dealing with now in your life?

Which issue brings up the strongest feelings for you?

What feelings does this issue bring up for you?

If those feelings had a color (or colors), what would it be?

Imagine that color filling the space in front of you so that it has depth, height, width, and aliveness.

Now watch that color swirl, congeal, and condense into a shape. Don't make it take a shape, just watch it and say the first thing that you see or that comes to your mind: An animal? Object? Plant? What? (If there is a problem coming up with an image ask, "If this issue were an animal, what would it be?)

Now remember how as a child you liked to pretend you were a teacher or a doctor? It's easy and fun for you to imagine that you are the shape that took form from your color and answer some questions I ask, saying the first thing that comes to your mind. If you wait too long to answer, that's not the character answering - that's YOU trying to figure out the right thing to say!

_____, would you please tell me about yourself and what you are doing?

(Character), what do you like most about yourself? What are your strengths?

(Character), what do you dislike most about yourself? Do you have weaknesses? What are they?

(Character), what aspect of _____ do you represent or most closely personify?

(Character), if you could be anywhere you wanted to be and take any form you desired, would you change? If so, how?

(Continue, answering as the transformed object, if it chose to change.)
\J

(Character), how would you score yourself 0-10, in each of the following six qualities: confidence, empathy, wisdom, acceptance, inner peace, and witnessing? Why?

Confidence, 0-10. Why?

Empathy, 0-10. Why?

Wisdom, 0-10. Why?

Acceptance, 0-10. Why?

Inner Peace, 0-10. Why?

Witnessing, 0-10. Why?

(Character), how would _____'s life be different if he/she naturally scored like you do in all six of these qualities all the time?

(Character), if you could live _____'s life for him/her, how would you live it differently?

(Character), if you could live _____'s waking life for him/her today, would you handle ____'s three life issues differently? If so, how?

(Character), what life issues would you focus on if you were in charge of _____'s life?

(Character), in what life situations would it be most beneficial for ____ to imagine that he/she is you, become you, and act as you would?

(Character), why do you think that you are in _____'s life?

(Character), do you have anything else you would like to say?

Thank you, (Character!) Now here are a couple of questions for _____:

What have you heard yourself say?

If this experience were a wake-up call from your life compass, what do you think it would be saying to you?

Appendix III: IDL Dream Interviewing Protocol

Joseph Dillard, LCSW, PhD

What are three fundamental life issues that you are dealing with now in your life?

Tell me a dream you remember. It can be an old one, a repetitive dream, a nightmare, or one that you're sure you understand.

Why do you think that you had this dream?

These are the characters in the dream, beside yourself...

If one character had something especially important to tell you, what would it be? (Do not choose yourself! Usually an antagonist, like a monster, or an object, like a house or fire, work best.)

Now remember how as a child you liked to pretend you were a teacher or a doctor? It's easy and fun for you to imagine that you are this or that character in your dream and answer some questions I ask, saying the first thing that comes to your mind. If you wait too long to answer, that's not the character answering - that's YOU trying to figure out the right thing to say!

_____ are you a character in _____'s dream?

(Character), look out at the world from your perspective and tell us what you see...

(Character), would you please tell me about yourself and what you are doing?

(Character), what do you like most about yourself? What are your strengths?

(Character), what do you dislike most about yourself? Do you have weaknesses? What are they?

(Character), what aspect of _____ do you represent or most closely personify?

(Character), if you could be anywhere you wanted to be and take any form you desired, would you change? If so, how?

104

(Continue, answering as the transformed object, if it chose to change.)\|

(Character), how would you score yourself 0-10, in each of the following six qualities: confidence, empathy, wisdom, acceptance, inner peace, and witnessing? Why?

Confidence, 0-10. Why?

Empathy, 0-10. Why?

Wisdom, 0-10. Why?

Acceptance, 0-10. Why?

Inner Peace, 0-10. Why?

Witnessing, 0-10. Why?

(Character), how would _____ 's life be different if he/she naturally scored like you do in all six of these qualities all the time?

(Character), if you could live _____ 's life for him/her, how would you live it differently?

(Character), if you could live _____ 's waking life for him/her today, would you handle ____ 's three life issues differently? If so, how?

(Character), what life issues would you focus on if you were in charge of _____ 's life?

(Character), in what life situations would it be most beneficial for ____ to imagine that he/she is you and act as you would?

(Character), why do you think that you are in _____ 's life?

(Character), why do you think _____ had this dream?

(Character), why do you think (some dream event happened) or (some character) was in the dream?

(Character), why should _____ pay any attention to what you have said? Aren't these just a projection of _____ 's own wishes and desires?

(Character), do you have anything else you would like to say?

Thank you, character! And now a couple questions for _____:

What have you heard yourself say?

If this experience were a wake-up call from your life compass, what do you think it would be saying to you?

Appendix IV: Interviewing a Physical Symptom

What are three fundamental life issues that you are dealing with now in your life?

Choose any physical symptom. How does it make you feel?

If that feeling had a color, what color would it be?

Imagine that color filling the space in front of you so that it has depth, height, width, and aliveness.

Now watch that color swirl, congeal, and condense into a shape. Don't make it take a shape, just watch it and say the first thing that you see or that comes to your mind: An animal? Object? Plant? What? (If there is a problem coming up with a character, choose some animal. What is it doing?)

Now remember how as a child you liked to pretend you were a teacher or a doctor? It's easy and fun for you to imagine that you are the _____ and answer some questions I ask, saying the first thing that comes to your mind. If you wait too long to answer, that's not the character answering - that's YOU trying to figure out the right thing to say!

"(Character,) would you please tell me what you look like and what you are doing?"

(Character), what do you like most about yourself? What are your strengths?

(Character), what do you dislike most about yourself? Do you have weaknesses? What are they?

(Character), what aspect of _____ do you represent or most closely personify?

(Character), if you could be anywhere you wanted to be and take any form you desired, would you change? If so, how?

(Continue, answering as the transformed object, if it chose to change.)
\|
(Character), how would you score yourself 0-10, in each of the following six qualities: confidence, empathy, wisdom, acceptance, inner peace, and

witnessing? Why?

Confidence, 0-10. Why?

Empathy, 0-10. Why?

Wisdom, 0-10. Why?

Acceptance, 0-10. Why?

Inner Peace, 0-10. Why?

Witnessing, 0-10. Why?

(Character), how would _____'s life be different if he/she naturally scored like you do in all six of these qualities all the time?

(Character), if you could live _____'s life for him/her, how would you live it differently?

(Character), if you could live _____'s waking life for him/her today, would you handle ____'s three life issues differently? If so, how?

1.
2.
3.

(Character), what life issues would you focus on if you were in charge of _____'s life?

1.
2.
3.

(Character), in what life situations would it be most beneficial for ____ to imagine that he/she is you, become you, and act as you would?

(Character), why do you think that you are in _____'s life?

(Character), do you have anything else you would like to say?

Thank you, (Character!) Now here are a couple of questions for _____:

108

What have you heard yourself say?

If this experience were a wake-up call from your life compass, what do you think it would be saying to you?

Appendix V: Working With Interview Recommendations

Look back over the interview and list the specific recommendations that were made:

1) Make a list of the recommendations in the interview.

2) Choose the ones that you want to work on.

3) Make a weekly chart to track your application daily, before you go to sleep.

4) Operationalize them.

(Write them in a way that change is measurable so that you can test the method. What will be done differently? When? Are you eating more of this, less of that? Are you thinking different thoughts? Are you feeling different things? Are you talking/acting in different ways to certain people? When? How? What is different?)

5) There will be some items you can check off if you've done them before you go to sleep. Other items will need to be rated on a zero to ten scale. How did you do? Rate yourself without criticism. For example, in one interview, Air made a number of suggestions:

I can become Air when I want to not be hungry. It claims that will help, since it doesn't eat.

If I am taking things personally I can become air; it's supposed to help.

Become air to become less mindless or thoughtless.

When having self-doubt, become Air.

Here is an example of how recommendations can be charted daily:

Became Air when:	M	T	W	Th	F	S	S
("v" = less; ^ = more)							
hungry	3x	5x	-	3x	4x	6x	-
result (more or less hunger)	v	v	^	v	v	v	^
personalizing	1x	-	-	1x	2x	-	-
result (more or less defensiveness)	v			v	v		
mindless	3x	1x	3x	-	-	1x	3x
result (more or less mindful)	^	^	^			^	^
self-doubt	-	-	3x	4x	-	3x	-
result (more or less confidence	^	^		^			

7) Share your results weekly with someone to create accountability. Have fun!

Some nights before you go to sleep read over the recommendations you choose to work on. Check off or score yourself 0-10 on how you did on each of the recommendations you choose to put into practice. Read the interview over several nights a week to incubate a non-drama alternative reality in your dreams improve problem-solving during your dreams, and better prepare you for tomorrow.

Find a partner or a support person, such as another person who you exchange interviews with or an IDL Coach or Practitioner. Exchange emails. Send a report each week on how you have done on applying your recommendations. Don't worry about perfection; just focus on making a game out of doing better!

If you only do a bit of this, no problem. You can come back to this format with successive interviews and over time, you will improve your ability to monitor your application of your recommendations.

Index

114

www.ingramcontent.com/pod-product-compliance
Lightning Source LLC
Chambersburg PA
CBHW070155290526
45789CB00002B/772